SUZANNE RE

10 REASONS
YOU DIDN'T WRITE AN
OUTSTANDING
OPINION

**IMPROVE YOUR OPINION WRITING ON THE
BAR PROFESSIONAL TRAINING COURSE**

PUBLISHED BY INSPIRED TO STUDY LTD

Also by Inspired to Study Ltd

How To Write a 1st Class Essay

7 Mistakes Students Don't Make in 1ST Class Dissertations.

All titles available in print and eBook on Amazon &
<u>www.inspiredtostudy.org</u>

SUZANNE REECE

10 REASONS
YOU DIDN'T WRITE AN
OUTSTANDING
OPINION

IMPROVE YOUR OPINION WRITING ON THE
BAR PROFESSIONAL TRAINING COURSE

PUBLISHED BY INSPIRED TO STUDY LTD

First published in Great Britain 2016
by Study Rhino Limited

Second publication in Great Britain 2017
By Inspired to Study Ltd
©Copyright Suzanne Reece

Print ISBN: 978-0-9955436-5-2
Electronic ISBN: 978-0-9955436-6-9

Inspired to
Study

DEDICATION

This book is dedicated to the memory of

Violet Reece.

She brought me into this world,

She protected me,

She taught me,

She loved me,

Mum

I will always love

YOU.

CONTENTS

FOREWORD

I have known Suzanne now for over 20 years and regard her as a dear friend. Our paths first crossed at what was then a well known national firm of solicitors and has since then grown into the large international practise of DACBeachcroft. There she specialised in personal and catastrophic injury work for many years. She is a very able and determined adversary who always put her clients' needs first. She is very much a results driven person and given that we both practised Law this was not a bad thing. She took all of that experience into teaching and training students who were to become young members of the Bar. Many years later I was fortunate enough to have one of her former students appear in front of me and she had nothing but praise for Suzanne. That praise was, however, tinged with the comment that students who attended her lectures never turned up ill prepared or offered the phrase "the dog ate my homework" as she is not one to suffer fools gladly. I was, therefore, surprised and humbled to be asked to write the foreword for this book. Knowing Suzanne as I do, this is an extremely important work to her as she wishes to pass on all her legal knowledge to help others achieve their potential.

Has she done this? Having read the book, I am in no doubt that she has. The book is written in a relaxed and easy flowing style making it user friendly and very accessible. Over the years I have dipped into my fair share of legal tomes (and still do) and wish all such books would think of the reader first as this book does. The book allows the reader to find their own style of learning using the R.E.D. technique. That is, "Read, Evaluate and Decide". Throughout the book Suzanne acknowledges this by referencing the fact that we all have different learning and reading styles. She does not say which one is better but encourages the reader to evaluate which is the best style for them whilst at the same time encouraging the use of structure and analysis. Added to this are exercises to emphasise the points being made and a thorough analysis of how an Opinion should be written from start to finish.

Suzanne identifies the key fundamentals that are essential to this process using the R.E.D. technique and follows this up with crucial advice to help the reader become an accomplished Opinion writer. See for example the five assumptions Suzanne refers to in the book set out below. These points should always be at the forefront of a student's mind:

1 "Don't accept everything you read, see, hear or do as right, correct or true.

2 Every witness or expert reflects his/her own values.

3 Publication doesn't mean it's right, correct or true.

4 You have the right to agree or disagree with any fact or opinion but you must explain why.

5 Your explanation should be logical".

I have no doubt that used properly this book will be an extremely important work in helping young Barristers of the future make the most of their abilities and ultimately provide the most consistent, thoughtful and helpful advice to their clients.

District Judge Paul Brooks
Central London and Bromley County Courts

30 August 2017

CHAPTER 1
INTRODUCTION

"The best preparation for tomorrow is doing your best today"

— H. JACKSON BROWN JR.

HAVE YOU EVER HAD so much information you cannot work out the right answer or even what to think? Have you ever felt that you are so confused you have no idea where to start to solve that opinion writing problem? Do you have all the law and cases in your head but it doesn't come out in opinion writing? Is it frustrating?

I was a City lawyer for over 17 years and a law lecturer for nearly 10 years, teaching students how to read and evaluate case papers on the BPTC. I would sit in my office and speak to students who, having read complicated case papers, could not work out how to write an opinion. I sat in my office one day speaking to a student, we will call him John Bull (you may have met him in your criminal case papers at City, University of London). He was a bright student but very frustrated with his performance. He had received a poor grade for opinion writing.

We discussed his opinion and how he had answered the mock assessment opinion. I then asked him a series of questions about the opinion problem. John answered my questions confidently and sure of his position. At the end of our discussion his conclusions to the opinion problem were entirely different from those he put in his opinion. John had all the legal knowledge he needed to answer the opinion question. His problem was that he did not understand the right questions to ask himself and how to record his thoughts in a logical way.

Do you ever feel that that despite working very hard at your legal research and having great legal knowledge on your topic you still don't write an outstanding opinion?

John looked at me as if I was a magician; the confusion had disappeared and he felt good. I reminded John that if he followed our approach to this problem he could apply it to any subject and any opinion he had to write in the future. John thanked me for my help but as he turned to leave, he asked if he could buy the book that explained this wonderful strategy.

Teaching trainee solicitors and law students for over 25 years has taught me how to help students to solve problems and get those outstanding grades. Years later the words of my students came back to me and I sat down and wrote this book.

What do you have to do? First, I want you to be committed to reading this book to the very end. Second, I also want you to commit to put in place the R.E.D. strategy for at least six weeks once you are on the BPTC. At the end of six weeks you will be studying more effectively and writing better opinions.

R.E.D. sets out our strategy for clear thinking and learning and stands for Read Evaluate and Decide. In this book you will find the tools to help you work out problems in a logical way with examples using the R.E.D strategy - think of the colour red.

Try to work through this book chapter by chapter and complete all the activities. You will learn by doing the activities as you read because this makes the learning more memorable. The early chapters of this book are about how you prepare to write your opinion; you may feel that you already know this information but read these chapters carefully as they form the preparation and basic understanding to help you eventually write your opinion. At the end of this book you will have a clear understanding why the R.E.D strategy is so important to help you identify and present clear arguments in your opinions.

I have one warning for you- this is NOT a law text book- you will not find any quotes from statutes, case law or discussion of legal principles. This book is written mainly for civil opinions but the general principles apply to criminal opinions. I expect you to have done the legal research, this book will help you convert that research into an outstanding opinion.

You want to write an outstanding opinion because you want to work as a barrister. You will write better opinions if you understand why in the real-world barristers are asked for a written opinion. Instructions to advise in writing will usually arrive from solicitors on behalf of their clients. Barristers can also be instructed directly by members of the public, other professionals, companies and non-corporate organisations.

Irrespective of the source of your instructions there is always a legal issue that requires your specific expertise. This legal expertise is rarely required in simple or straightforward problems so there is often an element of uncertainty on the issue you are being asked to consider because of the state of the law, case law, facts or evidence.

Barristers can be asked to advise in writing on many different areas of law ranging from family matters to commercial international disputes covering issues such as:

- Liability
- Damages

- Causation

- Evidential matters

- Interpretation of points of law

- Drafting claims, defences, applications, statements or affidavits

- Advising on specific applications, processes, proceedings or appeals

- Funding – either public funding or private funding from an insurer

- Settlements and negotiations

- Arbitration

- Trial preparation

- Commercial and tactical matters relating to a legal dispute

Your advice is often required to encompass financial, commercial and tactical considerations that have nothing to do with the law but are VERY important to your client. Your instructions should make these financial, commercial and tactical considerations clear. If you fail to address or advise on all your client's issues (legal and non-legal) in your written advice you have not done an outstanding job.

In addition, your advice will be required to consider the procedural position of your client's case and advise on what steps should be taken next. You need to have an excellent knowledge of the Civil Procedural Rules (CPR), Practice Directions (PD) and guidance, so the White Book (or the online version) should always be close to hand. Your advice will have to incorporate tactics and where appropriate settlement options. You will note that whilst you are asked for a legal opinion you work must cover a great deal more than just the law.

There is an old joke in the legal profession which asks: "If you have five lawyers in a room how many opinions will you have on the same question?" Answer - at least five! The point is that each lawyer will give you a different opinion. Think of some of the leading cases the Supreme Court has had to consider - there will have been at least two different and firmly held opinions on the same issue, one by each side. Each side would have obtained advice from a senior barrister, junior counsel and experienced solicitors on both sides. In a profession that is not a precise science it is acceptable for lawyers to come to different opinions. The effect is that it is acceptable for different students to come to different opinions in their advice and for both students to get outstanding grades. It is the process of how you apply the facts to the law and evidence; how you explain, conclude and write your opinion that is the basis on which your work will assessed. Keep in mind that different opinions on the same issue can both be right!

Finally, you are required to do something amazing ... look at the arguments or dispute from four different positions. First your client's position, second the position of your opponents, then the court or tribunal and finally you will consider YOUR own views. How you form your advice will depend on which party you are instructed to act for. In formulating your advice, you will have to understand your client's case, your opponents' position and how this undermines your client's case. You will also need to understand how the court is likely to approach the dispute using the CPRs, Practice Directions and guidance, should the matter go to court or a tribunal. You will need to think like a judge. You will need to assess how a judge will apply the CPRs or tribunal rules and how he/she is likely to exercise their judicial discretion. Finally, you will add in your own views.

Writing an opinion is never easy but when you are new to the skill of opinion writing it can be confusing. If you PRACTISE opinion writing it will get easier. Sit back relax and read!

Visit www.inspiredtostudy.org to download your FREE opinion planning infographics. Get further information on other books, webinars and workshops. If you intend to continue to masters level or beyond, my next book, *7 Mistakes Students Don't Make in 1st Class Dissertations*, will help you plan and write your next dissertation. Sign up to be notified of publication at www.inspiredtostudy.org.

◁ TOP TIP

Improve your opinion writing skills today
and your opinion grades
will get better
tomorrow.

CHAPTER 2
HOW DO YOU PREFER TO LEARN?

B EFORE YOU START TO UNDERSTAND why some students write an outstanding opinion I need you to understand some basic theory on how you learn. **If you are aware of how you learn it will help you understand your instructions and case papers.**

ADULT LEARNING SKILLS

Generally, it is accepted that adult learners have developed the following skills:

- They direct their **own study.**

- The **motivation for learning is internal** (you are in control!)

- They have **experiences** they can draw on to **help them learn**

- Learning is **driven by a need to know** (there is a problem to be solved or an opinion to write!)

- They are driven to **find solutions to problems** rather

than just gain information.[1]

LEARNING STYLES

Educational psychologists love to debate how learning styles develop and there are many theories. One theory is that adult students have three or four different learning styles that help them process information. During your studies you may use more than one learning style. You will usually have a personal preference for at least one style which is related to your personality and this is called your preferred learning style. Over time it is possible your preferred learning style may change. All types of learning styles are fine. How will you find your learning style? I will describe each learning style and you will recognise your own style, it will be obvious to you.

There are four major learning styles, easy ways of remembering them are:

VISUAL (seeing), **READING** (read & write), **HEARING** (aural), **DOING** (kinesthetic)

- **Visual learners** prefer to learn by seeing things performed, drawn or mapped out before their eyes. **'Seeing is believing' with visual learners, they remember what they have seen.**

---

[1] Fry, H, Ketteridge, S and Marshall, S (2003) A Handbook for Teaching and Learning in Higher Education.

9

- **Read and write learners** love reading and words. Often they are found sitting quietly reading. They like writing and often make lengthy notes. **'I have read'** says the read & write learner.

- Aural means hearing. **Hearing learners** like to learn by listening to what people say. They are busy listening but they also love talking and discussing problems so they can hear the solution. **'I hear you', says the hearing learner.**

- Kinesthetic means movement. **Kinesthetic learners** like to do things - they need movement and touch. **They learn by doing practical tasks**, building and making things. They are good at role playing. **'I made a proto-type and from that I discovered that'** ...says the doing learner.

@ACTIVITY No 1

Ask yourself – How do I prefer to learn? Tick your preferred style[s]

Remember that most students use several learning styles so you may have more than one preferred learning style.

VISUAL [ ]

READING [ ]

HEARING [ ]

DOING [ ]

The advantage of using your preferred learning style(s)

How you prefer to learn will indicate how you like to record information whilst you are studying. If you record information in your preferred learning style you are more likely to understand and retain that information. In short it makes studying easier for you.

How to Use Your Preferred Learning Style

VISUAL	READ	HEARING	DOING	Add your thoughts below
SOLUTION	SOLUTION	SOLUTION	SOLUTION	
Draw pictures, diagrams or time-lines to work out opinion questions -you need to see the problem.	You love every-thing printed so make sure you get a copy of the written lecture notes and all the printed slides and handouts	You listen and talk through problem solving - so find a study group and work with others who like discussions	You cannot simply sit at your desk so move around whilst you process the problem. You need frequent breaks so you can move	
Visualize your-self in the problem. Use visual aids such as Trello to help you chart your work. Turn words into pictures, charts or diagrams.	Write your own notes as this is how you learn. Use apps such as Evernote to keep your notes organ-ised.	Ask questions-and listen to the answers in group learning. Talk out loud and verbalise the problem. Talk out loud to hear the solutions if you are on your own!	Make models of the problem and try to model the solution and then write it down. Draw a wireframe or out-line the problem on a storyboard.	
Organise your work. It helps you to see the whole picture	Turn pictures and diagrams into words.	Listen to record-ings or webinars and lecturers. Find podcasts and listen to ra-dio debates on your topic.	Use modelling apps to see the practical prob-lem. Try Mind-Nodes, Coggle, Edraw or other online apps that help with story-boards and wireframes	

VISUAL	READ	HEARING	DOING	Add your thoughts below
SOLUTION	SOLUTION	SOLUTION	SOLUTION	
Express your answer in pictures before writing your answer	Your focus is the words you like to read silently so find a quiet place to study where you can focus on words	Use computer aids that talk to you	This kind of learning is great for physical tasks – such as learning physical skills, practical sciences or computer skills.	
Use lots of colour	Use highlighters when reading to make words stand out	Join a blog or social media discussion forum	If you have a physical object – hold it, touch it and try to work out a practical solution	
Use visual aids/ flow charts /maps	Read articles or blogs rather than watching video recordings	Dictate your thoughts using computer voice recognition software	If you do not have a physical object, then role play helps - get into role and find the solution	
Use different colour highlighters when reading and writing notes - make a memorable visual statement for your mind to remember	Revision for you is to reduce your lengthy notes into shorter memorable notes. Don't be tempted to simply browse through your notes	You like discussions but most assessment at some stage will be written so do not forget to write down your thoughts	Modelling and role play are great but don't forget to write the answer down.	

When you receive information in a format that is NOT your preferred learning style you often struggle to understand that information. This does not mean that you are not intelligent, it just means you must work a bit harder to put the information in a form that you prefer. If you understand that you are struggling with the format of the information rather than the legal knowledge, you should feel better able to power through those tough opinions questions!

Example

The Maths Haters and Lovers

I had law students who hated any form of maths or calculations. They hated having to work out financial schedules. They would convince themselves they could not answer questions presented in this way (even with a calculator). I spent a large part of the class convincing these students that the maths formulae were very simple and easy to work out. Other students loved calculations and could work out very complex legal problems in this format with great ease and apparent enjoyment! Both groups understood the law but those students who hated any form of calculations struggled to answer these questions in this format.

Do you like maths? No? Just put the question in a format or style you prefer and you will find it easier to understand. Think about it. If you prefer information visually convert that opinion question into a picture. If you are a "doing learner" set up a model of the question. Once you can understand the question you can work out the answer in a style you prefer. The final stage is to then turn your answer back into the format required, in our example a schedule or calculation. Hate maths? Picture or model the question, work out the answer and then turn that answer into figures.

You know your learning style and it is now time to put that knowledge to the test by starting to deal with the problems you have in writing an outstanding opinion. The reason you didn't write an outstanding opinion is that you failed to **READ, EVAL-UATE & DECIDE** (R.E.D.) on the main factual and legal issues. In the following chapters we will go through each main problem in detail and I will show you the solutions. Time to set out the ten problems:

10 REASONS
You Didn't Write
an Outstanding Opinion

1. You didn't **read** your instructions and case papers **PROPERLY**.

2. You didn't **identify** the **KEY** or important **facts**.

3. You didn't **identify ALL** the key factual and legal **problems**.

4. You didn't **understand** the arguments.

5. You didn't **think** like a barrister.

6. You didn't **evaluate** the law, facts, evidence and issues.

7. You didn't get the **right answers or express an opinion** on **key issues**.

8. You didn't set out your **reasoning and conclusions**.

9. You didn't have a **clear and logical structure**. You didn't give the right amount of **weight** to each issue.

10. You didn't write your opinion in a **language and style** appropriate for a professional opinion.

We start our problem solving with READING. In the next chapter I am going to show you 5 steps to help you find facts, evidence and information in your instructions and case papers.

THE 5 STEPS OF OPINION READING

THE 5 STEPS OF OPINION READING	
STEP 1	READ your instructions and case papers PROPERLY.
STEP 2	FIND the KEY FACTS.
STEP 3	FIND the GAPS in the FACTS.
STEP 4	FIND ALL the KEY factual and legal PROBLEMS.
STEP 5	FIND & SEPARATE the main ARGUMENTS.

☝ TOP TIP

If you know how you **prefer to learn**
You will **retain the information** you learn.

If you know how you **prefer to present** information
You will **present in a way you and others will understand.**

Chapter 3
Reading

REASON 1:
You didn't read your instructions and case papers properly.

I know you read the instructions and case papers before you started writing that opinion but the key word here is properly! The object of reading your instructions and case papers is to find all the key or important information, if you skipped over vital information you did not read your instructions and case papers properly.

Students who fail to read their instructions properly will only advise on some of the opinion questions. The effect is that their grades are limited to the part of the question they answered and they cannot get marks on topics or issues they did not address. To get full marks, you MUST ANSWER EVERY PART OF YOUR INSTRUCTIONS and make sure that you cover each part of the assessment criteria.

The Solution:
#STEP 1: Read your instructions and case papers
properly.

Let's start by recapping on the different types of reading:

1. **Superficial reading** – Here you just cover the basic outline so you may only read a couple of lines or paragraphs
   to understand the broad outline. This type of reading often involves skipping over a lot of detailed information.
   This type of reading is very fast but you don't read the
   detail.

2. **Double reading** – Here you read something superficially
   to get the basic outline and then you go back over the
   work and read it again. For example, you typically use
   this style when reading long opinion questions. This
   type of reading starts fast but slows down when you re-
   read the work. You may make notes on the second reading.

3. **Detailed reading** - Here you read every word and paragraph carefully and make a record as you read. This is a
   slow reading pace but typically you only read the work
   once and have a very detailed understanding of what you
   have read.

Superficial reading is fine if you are reading a menu at your fa-
vourite take-away café but it does not work for R.E.D learning.
**You cannot properly read, evaluate and decide if you have not
processed all the information; so double reading or detailed
reading is required for R.E.D.**

R.E.D. requires 'active reading'. This does not mean that you do press-ups as you read but your mind must be focused on the reading. How many times have you sat at your desk reading something only to find that five minutes later you have no idea what you just read? **The best way to actively read is by making some sort of record that reflects your learning style.** You choose how you want to record information. It may be a flow-chart, picture, grid-table, a list, voice recording or a written note. Simply reading without any form of record taking is the best way to fall asleep!

HOW TO FIND WHAT IS IMPORTANT IN YOUR INSTRUCTIONS AND CASE PAPERS

You do not need all the information you read in your instructions and case papers. Some information is helpful background information. Some information is key to understanding the legal problems. Some information has no purpose - it is just repetition or irrelevant to your advice. You find what you need in your reading by applying a few R.E.D. reading STEPS.

What Am I Asked to Do?

Read your instructions: they tell you what you need to resolve in your opinion. READ your instructions AGAIN and this time read every word. Look at the key words that convey the task you have been asked to complete. Are you being asked to explain, discuss, describe, advise or assess? Some students superficially read their instructions and think all the important information is in their case papers with the factual statements and evidence - they are wrong. Start with reading your instructions carefully: it is amazing what useful facts and information are included in your solicitors' instructions that may not be in the statements.

@ACTIVITY No 2

Do the words below all mean the same thing? Use your dictionary to look up and record the meaning of each word.

Explain ....

Discuss...

Advise ....

Assess ....

Evaluate...

The words above are asking you to do different tasks. Get them wrong and you are not accurately answering the question.

@ACTIVITY No. 3

Consider question A below. Set out broadly the areas the questions should cover. You do not need to be an expert in the subject area; just read the question carefully. Do not research any freedom of speech case law or legislation because this activity is not about your legal knowledge but how you would construct an answer.

Question A

In a democratic country, the state is required to protect the rights and views of groups that they do not agree with if those views do not breach any law. Describe the law on freedom of speech in England and Wales with two examples of its use in recent cases before the courts.

Write your answer here:

OUTLINE ANSWER TO ACTIVITY NO. 3

Freedom of speech

- Describe the laws on freedom of speech - generally
- Who is protected by the law?
- What is the extent of the protection under the law?
- When is the protection withdrawn? – (breach of criminal or civil laws on inciting hatred or violence)
- Example of recent case 1
- Example of recent case 2
- What do the 2 cases tell us about how the courts are interpreting freedom of speech laws?
- Discuss whether the recent cases support or refute the statement "...the state is required to protect the rights and views of groups that they do not agree with, as long as those views do not breach any law made in the question."
- Conclusion.

Look for the explicit questions you are asked to advise on and for those obvious questions that are **implied from the facts** that you have been given.

Example

> You are asked to advise on liability, quantum and evidence. You advise on liability and evidence really well

but if you forget to deal with an important item in assessing quantum you will not get full marks.

➢ You are asked to advise on quantum for general damages for a facial injury but there is also **on the facts and medical evidence** a potential and **obvious** claim for a head injury. A word of warning here: the key words are "evidence" and "obvious". Don't over speculate and try to find obscure medical conditions. Don't forget to advise in detail on your main area of instruction - the facial injury!

Record, in a style that suits your learning style, every question you are asked to address in your instruction and at the end of the opinion check you have covered every question. Tick or mark each question as done. Have you missed any? In later chapters on planning and writing your opinion we will discuss how to make sure this does not happen.

A great way of improving how you read your instructions is to look at past opinion papers that you have completed during the course and any mock assessment papers that are provided by your college or university. The more opinion instructions you read, the easier you will find working out what the opinion questions are asking you to do. Reading past opinion instructions on your core subject area is also good revision preparation for formal assessments.

¶ TOP TIP

"Success is no accident. It is hard work, perseverance, learning, studying, sacrifice and most of all, love of what you are doing or learning to do."

— Pele

READ. EVALUATE. DECIDE.

CHAPTER 4
FIND THE IMPORTANT FACTS IN YOUR READING

REASON 2:
YOU DIDN'T IDENTIFY THE KEY OR IMPORTANT FACTS.

The point of reading your instructions and case papers is to find the key or important facts so you can consider what the key factual and legal issues are when writing your legal opinion. If you cannot identify the key facts, you will have a problem in giving the correct advice.

The Solutions:
#STEP 2: Find the key facts

I thought I knew what facts were until I tried to describe them. I am sure you know what facts are? **A fact is '...a thing that is known or proved to be true.'**[2] Well, is that clear? Who proves that a fact is true or known? What happens if different people

---

[2] Oxforddictionaries.com

believe different facts? Facts are pretty slippery but it is your job to get hold of them. You must work out what facts are important, what they mean and where they came from.

An easy way of understanding facts is to picture the way you built a toy house as a child with toy bricks. You started with small heap of building bricks or blocks which you stacked up to build a house. These bricks or blocks are like our **facts - they are small bits of information** that you use to build much more complex structures. In the case of your opinion, **facts are what you use to build complex arguments and put forward conclusions and legal advice.** The way you use the facts will show that you have understood the area of law and will persuade your examiner to give you an outstanding grade.

FIND THE KEY FACTS USING THE BUILD A HOUSE METHOD

Continuing with our building comparison, when you build a house there are different functions for the building blocks. Some blocks are essential for erecting the house, for making it stable and water tight. A floor, walls, windows and a roof, these are essential for a house. There are other building blocks that are not essential they just add detail or decoration. These blocks that just decorate the windows, doors or the entrance are not essential for the building to be stable.

The key facts in your instructions and case papers are like the essential building blocks for the house. Without the key facts the arguments and conclusions in your opinion will not stack up or work. These are the main facts on which all other arguments and conclusions are based. In the build a house method you will find the key facts in your instructions and the early parts of your case papers and evidence before the more complicated evidence. Like the house, with the solid floor you will see these as soon as you walk into the house.

Build a house method

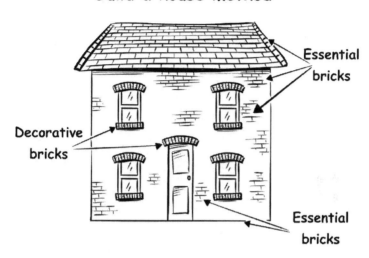

FIND THE KEY FACTS USING THE TELL A STORY METHOD

Another way to find key facts is to use the 'tell a story method'. The story starts at the beginning with the early information setting the scene and background information. The story progresses and more important information is added to the story until you get to the essential point of the story. The facts that are key to the story are not at the very beginning but somewhere buried in the middle of the story.

Unlike the build a house method, where we start with the key facts, in the tell a story method the key facts are in the middle of the story. They are not apparent at the beginning and often you must read some way into your case papers before it becomes clear what the key facts are. These key facts are often in witness statements or documents from several different people and you must unravel and collect all the key facts together.

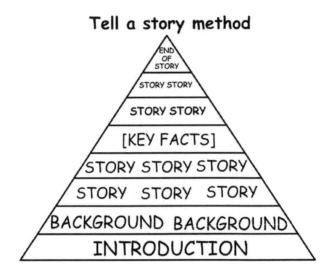

Your job is to work out what kind of structure (build a house or tell a story method) you have in your case papers – are the key facts up front at the beginning like the structure for the house or buried in the middle like a story? You must find the key facts.

HOW WILL YOU KNOW WHAT IS A KEY FACT?

Some students cannot work out what facts are important, which facts are just background facts and which facts are irrelevant. These students read their case papers and all the facts seem to be important. These students instead of picking out the key facts simply record and repeat everything they have read. A student, let's call him Stephen, put it like this – 'How do I know what facts I am looking for? When I am reading everything seems important.' We call this condition: 'I can't see the wood for the trees.' It means everything looks the same and I cannot see the most obvious thing in front of me. Sometimes you are looking at the detail and cannot see the bigger picture, you get so focused on the detail you miss the obvious. For example, you see the individual trees in the wood but don't spot that together they make up the wood. **Stand back and find the big picture, start with the obvious and then focus in on the detail.**

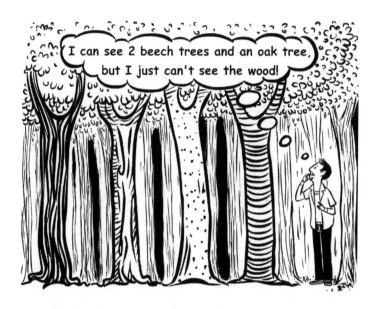

What Questions Help You Find the Key Facts

The facts that are important will depend on the questions that you are trying to solve. Go back to your instructions and case papers and ask yourself:

- What happened?

- When?
- Where?
- Why? - why did it happen?
- Who? - who was there? Who said…? Who got to the venue first?

If you can answer the 5 W's questions you will find the important facts in your instructions and case papers.

ANOTHER SOLUTION FOR PROBLEM 2:

#STEP 2a: Find the gaps in the facts

You have found the key facts in your instructions and case papers but sometimes important facts or information are missing. **If key facts or information are missing, then you only have part of the story. If you only have part of the story this will make the task of evaluating what you have read more difficult.** If you cannot find the missing facts or information you need to take this into account when evaluating what you have read.

Remember you are not looking for all gaps or missing information, you just need to spot the IMPORTANT missing facts and information. If the missing facts or information are minor or they are NOT important to understanding the 5 W's (what, when, where, why, who) that is ok - sometimes there is always some minor information that you don't have. If the gap in the facts relate to the 5 W's, then it will usually be important.

How to Find Gaps or Missing Facts

a) Look at the facts you have.

It is important for you to make a record of the key facts you have.

Look at them and ask yourself:

- What information is missing from the facts I have read?

- What further information should I have?

- Why is it missing?

- Where should I look for more facts?

- Who will know where to find the additional information? (or what other witnesses do I need?)

- Where is the document or person referred to by another witness or document that I have read?

- Do I need to see or hear something else? (Is there physical or audio evidence?)

b) Think like a detective

There is no secret formula - just use your common sense. Try to think like the person telling the story, who has recorded the information or provided the statement. Think about the facts you have and ask yourself: if I were a detective or in the secret service what other facts or information:

➢ **should I have** before I decide?

➢ would I **expect** to have been given to me?

➢ **would I have told** if this was my story?

Why You Need to Find the Missing Facts or Information

If you can identify that there is a gap, then you should be able to identify what fact or information is missing. If you know why a fact or information is missing, it may help you to understand where to look for the missing information. If you find the information, then you will have all the facts and information to come to clear decisions and conclusions in your opinion.

If You Cannot Find the Missing Facts or Information

If you cannot find the missing facts or information you will need to make it clear that your assessment or opinion is limited to the information you have read. This means that you present your conclusions as the views for the moment, they are provisional. Alternatively, your views may be subject to further information being obtained, so they are conditional. The advantage of this approach is that your examiner will recognise that you have spotted that IMPORTANT facts or information are missing. You should get marks for spotting that something was missing AND still advising your client even if it is a provisional or conditional conclusion.

READ. EVALUATE. DECIDE

¶ TOP TIP

Facts are everywhere

your job is to spot the

important

Facts!

CHAPTER 5
FIND ALL THE KEY PROBLEMS

REASON 3:
YOU DIDN'T IDENTIFY ALL THE KEY FACTUAL AND LEGAL PROBLEMS.

Reading your instructions and case papers should help you to identify the facts that are agreed, in dispute and that are missing. These facts with your legal research will then help you to identify what the important factual and legal issues will be in your opinion. If you cannot identify ALL the important factual and legal issues you will NOT give complete and comprehensive advice.

The Solution:
#STEP 3: Find ALL the KEY factual and legal PROBLEMS

The key facts should help you to identify ALL the key factual and legal problems to be resolved in your opinion. The key problems will depend on the questions you have been asked to address. Go back to your instructions and look at what you have been asked to do, remember how you recorded the key words, as it is time to focus on them again.

What you are looking for is the broad or general factual and legal problems that arise from the key facts. If you had to describe these problems in one or two sentences how would you describe them? Record them. The more complicated the opinion the more factual and legal problems there will be that need to be resolved. Your task here is to list ALL the problems in two lists: one for factual and the second for legal problems. At this stage do not worry about putting them into any specific order within the lists, just find them.

Once you have identified the key factual and legal issues it is time to start organising them within your lists. Start to group key factual issues that relate to each other together and then see if you can find a legal problem they relate to on the opposite side of the list. If you don't like lists - draw circles, graphs, pictures or group them in some other way you prefer.

Example

There is a dispute between A (a homeowner) and B (builder). There is disagreement between A and B on what was said and agreed at a meeting. They differ on two important points on the price.

A's case

- Price £5,000 no VAT(tax)

- Two payments of £2,500 over 28 days after completion.

B's case

- Price £5,000 plus VAT (tax)

- One payment due on completion.

You would group the two factual problems or dispute together (they both agree that payment was to be made in cash so this is not in dispute). This is one broad factual dispute about the price and payment terms. The two factual problems should relate to a legal problem on the opposite side of the list – what was the consideration for the contract and payment terms?

You know how to find the key factual and legal issues **the trick is to find them ALL if you want to write an outstanding opinion.** If you do not read your papers properly you will find some but not all the factual and legal issues. The answer is to make a careful record and to keep looking for all the key problems. Spend time thinking. We will look at how to plan and write your opinion in detail in later chapters.

The important point to remember is that this is the planning stage, you are reading and recording the important information in a style that suits your learning style. This is NOT the time for keeping important facts and problems in your head so record the information. If you are not recording the information you are not actively reading! If you are not actively reading you may fall asleep and miss an important problem you need to include in your opinion.

READ. EVALUATE. DECIDE.

¶ TOP TIP

"Learning is a treasure that will follow its owner everywhere."

— Chinese proverb

Chapter 6
Understanding the Arguments

REASON 4:
You didn't understand the arguments.

In the facts of every opinion writing exercise there are different arguments that can be put forward based on the facts, key problems and the law. Which arguments you choose to focus on will depend on which party you are instructed to act for and what you have been asked to advise on. To understand which arguments, you should focus on you must understand the key factual and legal arguments from four different positions:

1.   Your client's position

2.   Your opponents' position

3.   The likely position of the court or tribunal

4.   Your own position as the legal adviser

Before you can consider YOUR advice as the lawyer you should understand the three different positions in 1-3 above. You must **understand the factual and legal arguments being advanced for each key problem on your client's behalf, by your opponents and the position the court or tribunal is likely to take**.

The Solution:
#STEP 4: FIND and SEPARATE the main factual and legal ARGUMENTS.

How Do I Know What My Opponent's Position Will Be

First look at the procedural position, if there are proceedings there will be a statement of case setting out your opponent's position. If there are no proceedings look at the letter of claim or the reply to the letter claim for a detailed response to your client's case. In the early stages read the pre-action correspondence between the parties as this will usually set out the broad allegations made by your opponent.

How Do I Know What Will Be the Court or Tribunal's Position

The court or tribunal will in civil cases seek to apply the overriding objective set out in CPR 1 so make sure you are familiar with this important rule. Also look at specific procedural rules relevant to your client's dispute and for any guidance that has been issued by the court on how the rules and practice directions are to be applied. Specific types of work may also be subject to specific guidance issued by the court, for example, the Royal Courts of Justice has a Queen's Bench Guide[3]. The rules, practice directions and practice guides will give you insight into the orders the court can make and the factors they consider when exercising their judicial role.

FIND AND SEPARATE EACH MAIN ARGUMENT

Before you start to discuss different legal arguments you need to **find and understand each main factual and legal argument relevant to your opinion.** Use the same approach as you used for spotting the different factual and legal problems in the last chapter. Your job is to unwrap these arguments so that you can separate each argument before you can begin to take a more detailed look at them and compare them with each other.

How to Deal With Different Positions

It is difficult to eat spaghetti in one go so you should separate your spaghetti into smaller portions before you can attempt to eat it. This is also known as the "how to eat spaghetti" method. The way you tackle the different factual and legal arguments is by following a simple formula, it works every time, separate out your arguments.

1. **Give each argument a separate name.**
   Start by finding each argument and giving it a separate name.

2. **Make a record of the argument.**
   Make sure that whilst reading you record (in a style that suits your preferred learning style) the essential parts of

---

[3] You will not need to know the court guides for the BPTC assessment.

the argument.

3. **Only compare similar arguments on the same problem**.

    You should only compare similar arguments on the same problem. Look at your argument and your opponent's argument on the same disputed problem. In our earlier example of the building dispute between A and B this would mean comparing arguments on the payment of VAT (tax) with each other. Separately you would then consider the arguments on when payment was due that have been put forward by both sides.

4. **How is each argument similar to the other arguments**

    Now it is time to compare the different factual and legal arguments. Record where they agree.

5. **How is each key argument different from the arguments advanced by an opponent** Remember you may have more than one opponent.

    Now it is time to find the differences in the arguments. Record where one argument puts forward a position and the other is different or silent on the same point.

6. **Check out the evidence and case law for each argument**.

    Find and record what evidence or case law each argument is based on. Often one argument will rely on the court accepting one set of evidence whilst another argument on the same problem relies on a different interpretation or other evidence.

One position may rely on different or newer case law. You need to take this into account when comparing your arguments. The general rule is that decisions made by the higher courts are binding over the lower courts.

Supreme Court > beats > Court of Appeal

Court of Appeal > beats >High Court

High Court > beats County Court

Different decisions by courts at the same level have equal authority and must be distinguished on their facts until a decision on the same issues is given by a higher court.

Spend some time thinking.

You will have to spend time thinking about the information you have recorded. This is perfectly normal – take time to think things through and see, hear and find the big picture.

Your Objective

At the end of this process you should understand:

- the **key factual and legal arguments** that **support your client's case**.

- the key factual and legal arguments of **your opponent's case** (these undermine your client's case).

- How the different arguments for each party are **similar and different from each other**.

You should be able to summarise the above concisely in a style you prefer. If you can't then you have NOT understood the factual and legal arguments. It is time to go back and re-read the facts and evidence in your instructions and case papers. Having completed this exercise, if you are unsure of the law on which a legal argument is based it is time to do some more legal research on that area of law until you understand the legal argument.

Questions You Should Ask When Reading Your Instructions and Case Papers

Ask yourself the following questions:

A. Who do I act for?

B. What am I asked to do?

C. What are the key facts?

D. What are the key factual and legal problems?

E. What is the main area of law on each problem I must advise on?

F. How does the law apply to the facts AND evidence on each problem?

G. Are there any exceptions to the general legal principles I have applied?

H. Do the facts AND evidence fit any of these exceptions?

I. Do I have to calculate anything – where will I find the figures?

J. What is the current procedural position and what should happen next?

SUMMARY

Let's just recap on what you have done so far. You have started reading and identifying the key facts. You have identified the key factual and legal problems for discussion in your opinion. If you can identify the key factual and legal problems, it will help you to focus on understanding the different positions or arguments that may be advanced. Once you separate the different arguments, you will be able to compare them and see why and where they are different. You are doing more than simply recording and repeating information you have read. You are reading and critically thinking. Congratulations on completing the 5 steps of opinion reading.

READ. EVALUATE. DECIDE.

THE 5 STAGES OF OPINION READING	
STEP 1	READ your instructions and case papers PROPERLY.
STEP 2	FIND the KEY FACTS
STEP 3	FIND the GAPS in the FACTS
STEP 4	FIND ALL the KEY factual and legal PROBLEMS.
STEP 5	FIND & SEPARATE the main ARGUMENTS.

◁ TOP TIP

Sorting out your mixed up spaghetti
always makes it easier
to eat!

CHAPTER 7
THINK LIKE A BARRISTER

REASON 5:
YOU DIDN'T THINK LIKE A BARRISTER.

If you didn't approach writing your opinion with the right mindset you will not write an opinion like a professional lawyer.

The Solution:
 # STEP 5: Think like a Barrister

In the evaluation stage you are going to make decisions and judge the facts, evidence, law and supporting information you have recorded in the reading stage. In the evaluation stage you will need to think like a barrister and NOT like some students.

How Do Barristers Think

Barristers look at the facts, evidence, law and information from different positions. Remember in the earlier chapter you had to read and understand the arguments from four different positions:

- Your client's position

- Your opponent's position

- The position of the court or tribunal

- Your position as the legal adviser

In the evaluation stage you need to evaluate the facts, evidence and law from these four positions to work out your advice for your client.

Let me explain. A judge must listen to the arguments put forward by both sides and then he should look at the arguments from the position of the judge - fairly, impartially and independently. The referee in any game takes the same approach. The referee listens to the appeals made by both sides and then considers what he/she has heard or seen. They decide by applying the rules of the game. If they have help from any independent technology, they use this to help them decide. In tennis the umpire has 'hawk-eye' to replay a recording of the tennis ball bouncing near the play line which decides whether the ball was in or out. In international cricket matches the on-field umpires can refer close decisions to the off-field third umpire who has the benefit of a slow action video replay of the key point.

Barristers will take the same approach in considering difficult legal arguments. He/she will identify the problem, consider the existing arguments, carry out legal research, evaluate and produce reasoned arguments, draw conclusions and advise his/her client. In advising his/her client the barrister will look at the case from different positions to understand the strengths and weaknesses of his/her client's case. Your job is to think like a barrister.

THE 5 ASSUMPTIONS FOR THINKING LIKE A BARRISTER

Now that you understand the mindset you need let's start with some ground rules. We start with the FIVE assumptions which are the foundation of critical thinking in the evaluation stage. Remember your aim in writing your opinion is to find what is RIGHT, CORRECT or TRUE in your instructions and case papers. **The 5 assumptions make you challenge what you read, see, do or hear.**

The FIVE ASSUMPTIONS for thinking like a barrister are:

1. **Don't accept everything you read, see, hear or do as right, correct or true.**

2. **Every witness or expert reflects his/her own values.** Every witness or expert has their own personal beliefs, background, opinions, experiences and politics which make up their values. Their work is an expression and reflection of their values.

3. **Publication doesn't mean it's right, correct or true.** Just because someone has published facts or an opinion in a book, online, in the media, produced a report or published statistics does NOT mean they are right, correct or true.

4. **YOU have the RIGHT to agree or disagree** with **any FACT or OPINION** but you **MUST EXPLAIN WHY**.

5. **Your explanation should be LOGICAL.** You will provide a clear, sound, reasoned explanation for your opinion.

You Have Control

This is your opportunity to judge or assess the quality or value of the information you have collected. You will decide what worth, standard or weight is to be given to the facts, arguments, supporting information or data that you have read. How you think and evaluate is the whole reason you spent so much time reading and understanding your legal research, instructions and case papers. This is the time to think like a barrister. This is the part of your opinion that will separate you from other students and get your outstanding grade.

Don't Think Like a Weak Student

How do weak students think? Well they start with all the information they have gathered and they just want to write it down in an opinion as quickly as possible. They do not have time to think or evaluate what they have read.

They usually make a quick decision about the correct answer either before or during writing their opinion. These students sometimes work out they don't like their arguments whilst writing their opinion and change their conclusions as they go along. Some students never come to any decisions on key issues nor do they reach conclusions by the end of their opinion.

Don't Sit on the Fence

Imagine sitting on a fence, you are not on either side of the fence just perched awkwardly on top. Some students feel overwhelmed by the task of having to decide what worth, standard or weight is to be given to the facts, arguments and law they have read. They feel that they don't have enough experience or simply don't know enough about the subject to judge what they have read. They are wrong, go back to our five assumptions on evaluation and read them again. You will be required to get down off the fence and decide which side you are on.

The 50:50 student

Ok so we have dealt with students who don't like to make a decision but other students devise another solution to the problem which is just as bad. These students fear making the wrong decision so they always take the middle ground, they think this is the safest position. These students think that if they always stay in the middle then they have at least a 50:50 (50%) chance of getting the right answer as opposed to a 100% chance of getting it wrong, if they pick the wrong answer. They are not confident of getting the right answer so they make the calculation and bet in the middle. These opinion answers often sound very weak in their conclusions because they have failed to evaluate the strength and weaknesses of the arguments.

Example

A typical 50:50 opinion student answer would sound like this: "...there are good arguments for A... There are equally strong arguments for B... In conclusion both sides have valid arguments..." How do you feel reading that conclusion? What effect do you think this type of opinion will have on an examiner assessing your work? How do you think a future client will feel receiving this type of legal advice?

Both the 'sitting on the fence' and '50:50' strategies have the same results - they do not fool the examiner. All you are saying is: I don't know how to evaluate or assess what I have read. I don't know how to come to conclusions on what I have read. I don't want to decide because I am frightened I will get the wrong answer. These students may get a bare pass but they are never going to get an outstanding grade.

Just jump in and start taking control, have confidence and make a reasoned decision. Just take a 360 degree look around and form a view based on what you have read and the process of evaluation which we will consider in the next chapter.

READ. EVALUATE. DECIDE

◁ TOP TIP

"Quick decisions are unsafe decisions."

— **Sophocles,** ancient Greek playwright

CHAPTER 8

EVALUATION – PART 1 – THE PROCESS

REASON 6:
YOU DIDN'T EVALUATE THE LAW, FACTS, EVIDENCE AND ISSUES.

If you simply repeat the facts, cite the relevant law and evidence WITHOUT evaluating them and incorporating this into your advice; you will fail to demonstrate an outstanding application of the law to the facts and evidence.

The solution:
 # STEP 6: Follow the A-E stages of evaluation

Which are:

Stage A: Check your key facts are correct

Stage B: Find independent evidence and information to support your key facts

Stage C: Grade your main arguments

Stage D: Find the gaps in the main arguments

Stage E: Put your arguments in order

Stage A: Check your key facts are correct.

Make sure that you have made an accurate record of the key facts. It is important to state the key facts correctly. You lose marks if the facts are mis-stated, over-stated or inaccurate. Facts are the foundation of the arguments you will build for your opinion: get the facts wrong and you may end up with the wrong answer.

Stage B: Find independent evidence and information to support your key facts

You will try to find independent evidence and information that supports or confirms the key facts as being 'accurate, correct or true'. Facts can also be corroborated by other information such as witness statements, official records, verified data, verified research, documents, audio or image recordings – the list can be very long.

The general rule is that facts that are confirmed by independent or official records or data are less likely to be wrong. If you can support your facts with independent evidence, official records or data, then the arguments you make, based on those facts, are more likely to convince your examiner that they are accurate, correct or true.

When you cannot find supporting information for your key facts then these opinions move towards theory and speculation. They have less influence than arguments that are supported by independent evidence. You have to work harder to convince the

reader with your logic and reasoning that unsupported speculation is the right opinion. The task is not impossible but it is
harder.

Remember how to build your opinion answer

You start by identifying the key facts and understanding the key
factual and legal problems. You use the key facts which are supported by independent evidence and information (for example
documents, recordings, witness statements etc.) to start to develop factual and legal arguments. Your arguments help you
develop conclusions. Your conclusions form the basis of your
advice in your opinion.

At this stage you will have read your case papers and fully re-
searched the law. Here you will start to evaluate or assess the
quality of the main factual and legal arguments you are thinking
of using for your written opinion.

**Not all information has the same worth, quality or standard.
To help you evaluate or judge the strength or weakness of your
arguments, in the evaluation stage, it is necessary to work out
the 'worth,' 'quality' or 'standard' of the information you have.**

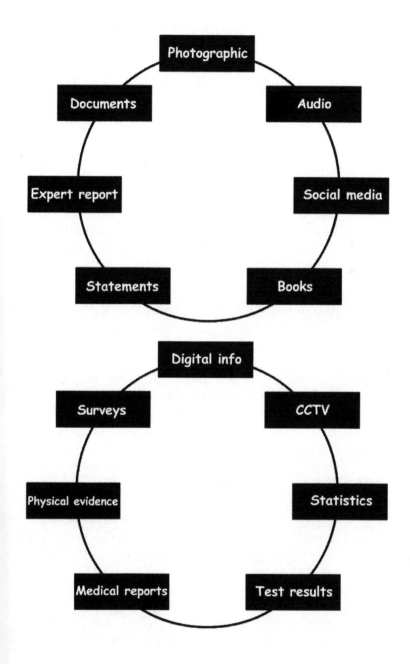

Independent and official evidence that has been verified or corroborated has good persuasive influence. What you are trying to do is to find facts and supporting information so that you can say, "look at this, it comes from a very good source, it has been checked and you can believe this."

Make a note of the source of your main facts and supporting information

To give value to facts and supporting information you need to record where the main information came from. Record this information as you read as you will need to review it later in the evaluation stage. This is NOT where you read the information. Here we are looking for something deeper: who or what specifically confirms the information as true, correct or accurate. What was the original source of the information?

Example

- You read a file containing three witness statements but the main statement for your case is by A Hornby dated 3 February 2016. You would record the name and date of this witness statement.

- You read a series of meteorological reports but the one that is important for your opinion is a specific report so you would record, for example, the meteorological report dated 4 June 2016 for the London area as the source of the key facts relating to the weather conditions on that day.

- In a commercial dispute you are asked to advise on the law; you have read a copy of solicitor's file but the specific document related to the terms of the dispute is the contract dated 21 March 2014 between Tech2000 and Smith-Palmston Plc, this is the document to record.

Let's recap: The A-E stages to evaluation - you have completed A & B stages of evaluation.

A. **Check your key facts are correct** ✓
B. **Find independent evidence and information to support your key facts** ✓
C. Grade your main arguments
D. Find the gaps in the main arguments
E. Put your arguments in order

Stage C: Grade your main arguments

How to grade the facts and supporting information

Your reading of your instructions and case papers should have given you the key facts, supporting evidence and information. You should have identified at least one main argument (based on the factual and legal issues) that supports your client's case (often you will have more than one). You should also have at least one argument that will be used by your opponent to undermine your client's case. Your job is to evaluate the strength and weaknesses of the main arguments.

First you will evaluate the strength of your client's main argument (or main arguments where you have several). Second you will compare and evaluate your client's arguments against your opponents' arguments on the same issue.

The Grading System

Remember this is not a precise mathematical equation. You can either score using numbers between one and five or a grade from very poor to very good. I prefer to use the grade approach. **Give the main facts and supporting evidence for each main argument a score or grade.**

Scoring system for evaluation

One = very poor

Two = poor

Three = neutral (neither poor nor good)[4]

Four = good

Five = very good

Example 1

Let's assume there was a serious car crash on a motorway late at night. No other cars were involved in the accident and the driver was not hurt. There are two potential reasons why the car crashed: either the driver lost control or there was some mechanical defect with the car. There is no dispute that the car crashed (fact one). Assume there is conflicting information about the cause of the crash (fact two). Treat the facts about the cause of the crash (fact two) as if they were on different sides of a game and value the supporting information to support each cause separately. Once you have graded the two potential

---

[4] Sometimes after a proper evaluation there are arguments that are equally balanced but this is not the 50:50 approach or sitting on the fence; as you will be able to explain your conclusions based on the facts, evidence and law.

causes of the crash you will have two grades, one for each version of the disputed fact.

Fact one - the car crashed, there is no dispute over this.

Fact two - the cause of the crash was either:

A - the driver lost control or

B - there was a mechanical problem with the car.

The supporting evidence:

The driver says the car's steering, power and controls malfunctioned; this supports argument B. You also read a mechanical report from the insurers of the car which states the car was in good working order before the crash and had no defects; this supports argument A; the accident was the driver's fault. Your job is to assess the evidence of the driver and the mechanical report. Let me show you how to do this.

Argument B requires you to assess whether the driver is a good reliable source of information. Do you believe his evidence that the car controls malfunctioned? Let's say you take the view his version is plausible and you have nothing to indicate he is not telling the truth. There is no independent evidence to corroborate his version of events. All you have is his statement so you judge him – grade him neutral (his evidence is plausible); if you believe his recollection is convincing, grade his version as good.

Argument A – the accident was the driver's fault. You have a mechanical report carried out by an independent and qualified expert who thoroughly tested the car; you would grade this evidence as very good because this evidence is from an independent and impartial source. The engineer has no personal interest in the finding and results of the inspection, he has no reason to misrepresent his test findings. The result is that argument A wins over argument B. The more likely cause of the accident was that the driver lost control as the mechanical report shows the car was in good working order before the crash.

Example 2

Would my answer be different if there were two credible witnesses who were passengers in the vehicle, unrelated to the driver? Both passengers confirmed that suddenly and without warning the vehicle failed to respond to the brakes or steering controls? YES. Now version B would be graded very good (The case has independent corroboration from two credible witnesses). The expert's report remains graded very good. Evaluating the evidence would lead you to the conclusion that both versions of events are credible; this is a case that would be determined on which witness (the expert or the factual witnesses) were better under cross-examination at trial[5].

Example 3

Here we have similar facts but this time the driver was tested at the accident scene and found to be twice over the alcohol limit for driving. He was convicted of driving with excess alcohol and banned from driving for two years. There were no witnesses to the incident and he had no passengers in the vehicle. You have

---

[5] This is NOT a sitting on the fence or a 50:50 decision because you have evaluated the evidence and can explain the reasons for your decision based on the facts, evidence and law!

a mechanical expert's report as set out above. Has your evaluation changed? Yes. Now the driver's version of event is graded poor. His recollection of events is impaired by the level of alcohol he consumed and he has a strong reason for not telling the truth. The expert's report evaluation remains very good. Your evaluation would be that the likely cause of the accident was driver error due to alcohol intoxication[6].

I hope you see how evaluation of the same basic facts can produce different answers depending on how you evaluated the evidence and supporting information; it is a sliding scale and you must decide where is the correct position on that scale.

What do you do now? Nothing, just keep your grading of the arguments as a provisional valuation. This is not the end of the assessment: you need to move to the next stage, working out if there are any gaps in your facts or supporting evidence.

There are five stages of evaluation and you have completed the first three stages.

A. **Check your key facts are correct** ✓

B. **Find independent evidence and information to support your key facts** ✓

C. **Grade your main arguments** ✓

D. Find the gaps in the main arguments

E. Put your arguments in order

---

[6] A criminal conviction for driving over the alcohol limit when pleaded reverses the burden of proof in civil cases on this issue. These are advanced rules of evidence which for demonstrating this example you do not need to consider.

> ⌐ TOP TIP
>
> "The purpose of education is to replace an empty mind with an open one."
>
> — Malcolm Forbes

CHAPTER 9
EVALUATION – PART 2 - THE PROCESS

P ART OF THE PROCESS OF EVALUATING YOUR CASE is to work out if there are any weaknesses with the information you have. This usually means finding out if some IMPORTANT fact or information that you need to make an argument or decision is missing. In this chapter we will look at how to find important missing information and what to do if you cannot find it at stages D and E of evaluation.

Stage D: Find and evaluate any gaps in the MAIN ARGUMENTS

You found the gaps in the facts earlier when we looked at #STEP 2a: find the gaps in the facts on pages 30-31. Look at your record and you will take this one stage further. Think about the gaps in the set of facts and supporting evidence and information that make up the MAIN arguments for your opinion. **For each of the main arguments you are going to test them to see if there are any more gaps.**

How to find the gaps in the main arguments

Think about the facts and supporting information you have from all your different sources. Ask yourself: if I were senior counsel what other facts or information:

> **should I have** before I decide?

> **would I expect** to have been given?

> **would I have told** if this was my story?

Here there is no secret formula. Just use your common sense. Go back to the diagram on page 55 showing the sources of information; look at each source of information and ask yourself: "Should I have information from this source?"

Is the gap in the main arguments important

You have found a gap - now it is time to assess how important that gap is to your opinion. You are only concerned with IMPORTANT gaps in the main facts, supporting information and main arguments. If the gaps in the main arguments are trivial or un-important you may mention them but it will not change the strength or merit of your arguments.

If the gap is important then it is time to re-evaluate those arguments. If the gap is in one of the main problem areas you are trying to resolve in your opinion, then it is important. The more important the gap in the facts or supporting information the weaker the main arguments will be.

Does the gap weaken the argument

If a gap in the facts or supporting information is important it will nearly always weaken any position, argument or opinion on which it is based. It is time to re-evaluate your original grade for this main argument, usually by reducing the grade. Give it a revised grade between very poor and good or a revised score between 1- 4 if you are using the number method.

There are stages A-E of evaluation and you have completed stages A-D.

> A. **Check your key facts are correct** ✓
>
> B. **Find independent evidence and information to support your key facts** ✓
>
> C. **Grade your main arguments** ✓
>
> D. **Find the gaps in the main arguments** ✓
>
> E. Put your arguments in order.

You have checked your facts are correct, found supporting evidence and information that corroborates those facts, graded your main arguments and found any important gaps in your main arguments. Now it is time to put your arguments in order.

Stage E: Put your arguments in order.

Having assessed the quality of your client's main arguments it is now time to put the different arguments into some sort of order. Put the arguments in order with the best arguments on top going down to the weaker arguments at the bottom. On top are the arguments that you gave your highest grade or score. Remember, the best arguments will also depend on which side you are representing and what you have been asked to do. Do not include arguments that you have rejected at the evaluation stage as having no merit.

You will put your arguments in an order that support your client's case with the best argument on top and then going downwards with the weaker arguments. You will repeat the exercise for your opponent's arguments (those arguments that undermine your case). You will check that you have a counter-argument for ALL your opponent's arguments. If there are no facts in your client's case that allow you to formulate a counter-argument DON'T make one up (warning: if you do, this is a serious misconduct issue). You will have to advise your client that further information is required and this may be a potential weakness in their case.

Spend time thinking

Evaluation is something that requires you to spend time THINKING, take that time. Do the thinking now and save time when you start to write your opinion. Thinking now at the evaluation stage will avoid that awful feeling that you don't know what to think, what to write or what to conclude when you start writing your opinion. Evaluation requires you to stop writing and to start thinking. With proper evaluation you will be able to write opinions that have concise and logical conclusions

Congratulations you have completed ALL the stages!

Stage A: Check your key facts are correct ✓

Stage B: Find independent evidence and information to support your key facts ✓

Stage C: Grade your main arguments ✓

Stage D: Find the gaps in the main arguments ✓

Stage E: Put your arguments in order ✓

READ. EVALUATE. DECIDE

¶ TOP TIP

"The important thing is not to stop questioning."

— Albert Einstein

CHAPTER 10
MAKE YOUR OWN DECISIONS AND FIND YOUR OPINION

REASON 7:
YOU DIDN'T GET THE RIGHT ANSWERS OR EXPRESS AN OPINION ON KEY ISSUES.

The students think there is only one correct answer and their biggest fear is that they will get the wrong answer. Some students desperately quiz their friends after an examination to see if they wrote the same answer and get really confused when two students with different conclusions both get outstanding grades. Is that fair? Yes.

Students are frustrated when they are told they did not set out their views on the issues. They are confused when they look at their work and see that they repeated the relevant facts and law - did they have to do more? YES. You need to express YOUR opinion on key issues to write an outstanding opinion.

The Solution:
STEP 7: Get the correct range of answers AND express YOUR opinion on key issues

If you can understand how you build an opinion answer it is much easier to understand what you need to put into that opinion. You start with reading and from that you can identify the key facts and understand the key factual and legal problems. You use the key facts which are supported by independent evidence and other information to start to develop factual and legal arguments that support your client's case. Your arguments help you develop conclusions. Your conclusions form the basis of your written advice.

I often explained to my law students that examiners were not simply testing their memory or their ability to repeat facts. The purpose of assessing students' written opinions is to test how they have assessed the facts, supporting information and evidence. We want to see how students deal with the legal problems, justified arguments and came to conclusions. Examiners want to see how students assess and critically evaluate all the information they have and whether they correctly advised their client within the range of correct answers. This is the same approach all examiners take when marking an opinion in any subject.

TRY THE PLAYING FIELD APPROACH
The big secret is that examiners are not looking for one single correct answer. There is a range of correct answers and you can persuade your examiner with great factual and legal arguments that your answer is within the range of correct answers.

If your answer is in the right range you can obtain very competent marks. If you address ALL factual and legal problems with the correct range of answers you can get an outstanding grade.

Try to think of this problem as if it was a playing field for a sport such as netball or football. Let's divide the field into three sections and give each section of the field a colour. The red zone is the area with the wrong answers, you need to avoid this zone. Hit any of the wrong answers and you automatically go into the red zone. In this zone, for example, you got some fundamental understanding of the law, facts or legal arguments wrong. There is worse to come: within the red zone there is an area where you get an important or critical point wrong. This is the zone of red light fails where although you achieved the pass marks you still fail because:

A. Your legal or other analysis is clearly wrong and:

- You put your client's interests at risk;
- You are placed [as a potential barrister] at risk of liability for negligence or a disciplinary finding;

Or

B. Your work is so poor that it would:

- render no valuable service to a client and/or
- Put your client's interests at risk and/or

Place you [as a potential barrister] at risk of liability for negligence or a disciplinary finding.

The blue zone is mid-field and neutral territory. Here your overall advice is ok. In the blue zone you get a competent grade.

This tends to be where you demonstrate you understood the key problems and applied the correct law but your application, evaluation or analysis of the case needs further improvement. For example, you applied the correct law to the facts but your practical advice was weak.

The final area is the green zone, this is the area where a range of answers are correct and you obtain very competent and outstanding marks. Your objective is to get your opinion answers in the green zone and to address ALL the factual and legal issues so you get an outstanding grade.

PLAYING FIELD APPROACH

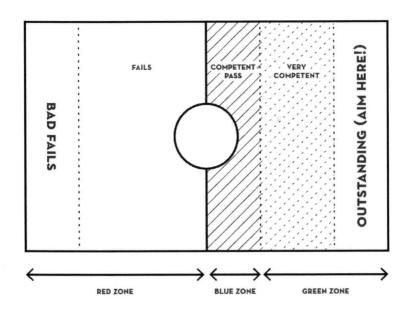

This is the **DECISION STAGE** of R.E.D. **Check you have the correct range of answers on all factual and legal issues**. The last stage is your chance to make a final check and adjustments to your work. The purpose is to check you have not omitted to consider something important. Think of this stage like checking your math after you have worked out that complicated algebra equation. Students often think they can miss this stage out if they have been thorough in the earlier stages - don't be tempted to do this.

The way you perceive a problem develops as you read more information and begin to evaluate the evidence and supporting information. As you develop your understanding of the arguments being made you get better at comparing the similarities and differences between arguments. It is easy to miss a key problem or fail to understand the importance of an issue in your early reading.

The review stage is NOT your chance to repeat the R.E.D. process but it IS TIME to do a quick CHECK. Many good opinions have been turned into outstanding opinions at this stage by spotting an obvious mistake, omission or error. Go back over your notes making sure you have covered the 6 STEPS:

The final review- The process

➢ READ your instructions and case papers PROPERLY. Have you answered ALL the questions you have been asked to advise on in your opinion? If there is more than one question or several parts to one question, check you have answered every part of the question. If you want maximum marks the easiest way to do this is make sure you get marks for every part of the question you are advising on.

➢ FIND the KEY FACTS.
Did you find ALL the key facts? Check your notes that you have not missed a key fact, as this may affect your evaluation. If your review shows you have missed a key fact, then go back and work it into your evaluation.

➢ FIND the GAPS in the FACTS.
Make sure you have found the IMPORTANT GAPS and check that you have not simply failed to read a fact. If you find new information or facts, go back and work them into your evaluation.

➢ FIND ALL the KEY factual and legal PROBLEMS
These are derived from the key facts, this is thinking time so put down your pen, close your tablet or note-book and THINK. **Have you left out a key issue?** Write down in bullet points the key problems as you see them now; now look at your earlier record of the key problems - are they the same? If you have missed a key problem, go back and work it into your evaluation.

➢ FIND and SEPARATE the main ARGUMENTS
You have sorted out **your arguments: make sure that you have them straight in your mind**. If you are clear in your thoughts, your arguments in your opinion will also be clear. If you are clear on your arguments writing your opinion will be much easier.

➢ EVALUATE the facts and arguments. **Check that you have got your main arguments in the correct order**.

The final part of getting into the right zone for an outstanding opinion is making your own decisions and finding YOUR own opinion. You do this in two ways: –

- by making decisions on key problems (which you did above)
- and by adding YOUR opinion on these problems.

YOUR opinion is important - time to add in YOUR assessments

You have concluded on all key factual and legal problems and reached an overall conclusion but you are not done yet. **The best way to write an outstanding opinion is to add in your own view or interpretation on the facts and information you have read.** Remember there were four positions to consider - you looked at the case from the position of your client, your opponents, the judge or tribunal and now it is time to think about that fourth position: -

- YOUR opinion on how the **court or tribunal** will decide disputed issues between the parties.

- YOUR opinion on the **prospects for success**.

- YOUR opinion on what **procedural, evidential and next steps** your client should take.

Having the ability to look at the facts, evidence and information from different points of view (client, opponent, judge and your own views) is important because it shows that you have understood the key issues. When you evaluate what you have read AND add your own opinion to the discussion you show your intellectual ability. When you incorporate YOUR own views you add legal expertise to the opinion. In short, this additional thinking and expression sorts out the outstanding students from the very competent.

Questions that you should ask to help you find YOUR opinion on ALL issues

1. What is MY legal advice on the law?

2. What is MY opinion on how the law applies to the facts of this case?

3. What factual and legal arguments will I use to support MY advice?

4. Is there the possibility that my opponents will have a different opinion?

5. What arguments will my opponents use to undermine MY arguments and why?

6. If the court or tribunal decides, what orders can they make?

7. What is MY opinion on how the court will decide this issue?

8. Explain why?

9. What is MY assessment of the prospects for success for my client's claim or legal issue (expressed as a percentage and in words)?

10. What is MY advice on procedure, evidence and the next steps to be taken?

THE PROSPECTS FOR SUCCESS

Your instructing solicitors will usually want some assessments of the prospects of success of the claim or legal dispute, if the matter is pursued. Remember you are asked for your advice and you should never start by pre-judging the facts, evidence and law before you have completely read and evaluated the evidence. You must make your own decision so forget any views expressed by anyone else. You will have to decide on the prospects of success which you should clearly express in words (and in a percentage).

Remember in civil cases the court must be persuaded on the balance of probabilities, this means 51% or more, to find in favour of a party. If a case falls below this standard it is your job to advise your client that their case is likely to fail or as we put it in the profession - there are poor prospects of success. If you decide the case is likely to succeed (it is likely to persuade a civil court or tribunal on the balance of probability) you will need to go on and advise your client on the strength of their case given all the evidence.

Each case is decided on its own facts, evidence and law but as a guide here are some general guidelines:

GENERAL GUIDELINES	
GUIDE-LINE 1	No case is ever guaranteed to succeed so never make a 100% assessment[7].
GUIDE-LINE 2	Very good prospects of success - 75% and above
GUIDE-LINE 3	Good prospects of success 60 - 75%
GUIDE-LINE 4	Reasonable prospects of success - 51- 60%
GUIDE-LINE 5	Marginal prospects of success - 50% (theses are cases that could go either way 50:50)
GUIDE-LINE 6	Poor prospects of success - less than 50%

What Happens When Your Client Has No Case in Law

Some students think there must always be an arguable case for their client. They think they just should look harder at the facts or make some big assumptions about the evidence they have or may get in the future to construct a case. You MUST always look for an arguable case for your client based on the law, facts and evidence you have. If your client's instructions are that further evidence may be obtained you may take this into account. You cannot make up facts or evidence that has no foundation in your client's instructions because it would help your client's case.

Sometimes, no matter how you look at the facts, evidence and law your client does NOT have a case in law. Your job, having

---

[7] Even where there is an admission of liability there can still be a dispute on causation and quantum. A claim is only guaranteed 100% when the parties have reached a binding agreement (and if necessary that has been approved by the court or tribunal).

assessed the facts, evidence and law, is to advise your client of the regrettable news.

Example

Raj has a vintage ford car that has not been working properly, he is no expert but thinks the engine has a problem. His friend Ravinder has just started a mechanical engineering apprenticeship, he started last week. Ravinder offers to have a look at the car as a favour because they are friends and he tells Raj "Mate I am not sure if I can fix it but I will take a look. I don't have any experience of fixing engines but what are mates for but to help out." There is no agreement that Ravinder will be paid for his time working on the engine. Ravinder looks at the engine and decides that it is far too complicated for him to fix. He decides he does not have the time and wants to focus on his apprenticeship and returns the car to Raj in the same condition.

Raj is annoyed that the engine has not been repaired. He instructs solicitors to sue Ravinder for breach of contract. Raj takes the car to a garage and pays £3,000 for the engine to be replaced.

You are instructed to advise in writing on whether Raj has a claim for breach of contract. Raj accepts that no money was agreed for the work but thinks Ravinder should be accountable because he broke his promise to fix the engine. Raj feels Ravinder could have fixed the car if he had spent less time watching cricket.

On Raj's version of events there are two essential elements to establish a contract that are missing. There was no intention to create legal relations and no consideration – here there is no contract and no cause of action in law.

Cases where there are poor prospects of success

Do not confuse a case where there is no cause of action in law with a case that is weak because of the facts or evidence. In these cases, you will find sufficient facts to make an arguable case in law but the facts and evidence make YOUR assessment of the prospects of success poor.

Example

Using the previous example of Raj and Ravinder let's change the facts. You act for Raj. Ravinder has his own garage and was experienced at repairing Ford car engines. He agreed to fix the engine at a discount as Raj was a friend for £200. He took the car and later returned it saying the engine had been fixed.

Raj says the car was returned with the engine still having the same problem before the purported repair. Ravinder claims the engine needed to be replaced and he could only do a temporary repair for £200. Ravinder says he told Raj the engine needed to be replaced but Raj wanted it patched up and he did this. Raj accepts that the repairs were never going to last for very long but claims they were never done. He took the car to a different garage and they replaced the engine for £3,000 because they said the engine was too old to repair.

On the above facts there is an arguable case that the temporary repairs were never carried out on Raj's version of events and therefore a case for breach of contract. There is conflicting evidence between the parties as to whether the repairs were carried out. The court is more likely to accept the evidence of Ravinder, an experienced mechanic, that he did carry out the work but that some other part of the old engine failed and that is why the engine did not work for very long after the repair. The evidence of your client's garage that the engine was old and beyond repair would support this view. On the evidence you have this is likely to be a case with poor prospects of success. Here the facts and evidence makes the case weak.

You now understand how to read, evaluate and form your advice on all the key issues, it is time to think how you are going to explain YOUR reasoning and conclusions in the next chapter.

READ. EVALUATE. DECIDE

꧁ TOP TIP

"If you can't explain it simply, you don't understand it well enough."

— **Albert Einstein**

CHAPTER 11
REASONS AND CONCLUSIONS

REASON 8:
YOU DIDN'T SET OUT YOUR REASONING AND CONCLUSIONS.

You may have done the legal research, reading and thinking about your written advice but if you didn't explain your reasons for forming your advice or how and why you concluded as you did, you will NOT get an outstanding grade. **Remember the purpose of the written advice is that your instructing solicitors and your client can understand how and why you advised as you did.**

The Solution:
STEP 8: Explain your reasoning and conclusions for all key arguments.

Summarise and Conclude on All Main Issues

Try to see these conclusions on the key factual and legal problems as a trail of stepping stones that leads the examiner from the beginning to the end of the opinion. **Each key issue must be discussed and at the end of each topic or problem there should be a conclusion.** Each new issue should be a stepping stone to the next topic or problem and eventually to the final conclusion at the end of the opinion.

Imagine you are walking across a small river. There are a series of stepping stones that forms a path across the water. Have you ever missed a stepping stone? Don't lose your examiner by missing out any of the stepping stones to your final conclusion. Allow the examiner to see a clear path along the stepping stones until the end. You will not gain marks in your opinion if the examiner cannot follow your arguments, reasoning and conclusions to the end of the opinion.

Another way of thinking about this process is to imagine you are playing a game of rounders or baseball at school – the object is to get around the pitch touching in at each base until you get to the end, TAKING THE EXAMINER WITH YOU. You want to make sure that the examiner has a summary and conclusion at the end of each main issue, like you are touching base as you move around the pitch. At the final base, you will have your final conclusion.

If you have summarised and concluded, at the end of each main issue your examiner will understand your reasoning and decisions. When the examiner has been carefully led through your opinion to the final conclusion you have accomplished one of the main features of an outstanding opinion: a clear and logical structure. The type of opinion that gets the highest marks are those that present the correct law, arguments and supporting information in a logical and well-structured written advice.

A Final Conclusion

Well the good news is there is always a final conclusion either in the summary of advice or in the conclusion at the end of the opinion. Remember, this is not a repetition of your discussion in the main body of the opinion; it is a brief summary with a final decision that answers your instructions. When you have written the final conclusion test it out, read it. Does your advice sum up concisely?

Remember, a conclusion is not your opportunity to repeat the arguments in the body of the opinion. **Your conclusion must be brief BUT not so brief that, having read it, the examiner is unclear why you have concluded as you have done.** Conclude and put in a brief explanation that justifies your conclusions. What have I just done? Repeated the same point several times; don't do this in your opinion conclusion.

The final conclusion should not be a surprise. Your arguments or discussion in the main body of the opinion should be consistent with the arguments and evaluations you have made earlier in your opinion. You make sure you are consistent by making decisions on all important issues before you start writing and making an opinion plan.

Make an Opinion Plan

Every good opinion starts with a plan. Don't have time for a plan? – trust me on this - a good plan will make writing your opinion so much quicker. As the old saying goes – 'preparation, preparation, preparation…fail to prepare and prepare to fail!' You will find that it helps to make a summary of your final decisions and main arguments in your opinion plan.

You should write an opinion plan, in a style that fits your learning style. Some students will draw a map or diagram; others may have a written list or a picture. Whatever your preferred learning style you must commit your opinion plan to some physical form that you can use. **Whatever method of record you choose for your opinion plan it should NOT be kept in your head because once you start writing it will disappear!**

Use your Opinion Plan

Head plans often get confused, lost or worse disappear when you begin to write your opinion. Record your plan and update it if you find new information. **Use your opinion plan as a guide** when you start to write or type your opinion. Keep referring to your plan as your writing progresses, it is a tool to help you, not something that you record and then leave under your laptop or a pile of books. **Your plan keeps you on track and makes sure you don't miss important topics you identified in the earlier stages**, tick off sections that you have completed as you progress. Use your plan.

READ. EVALUATE. DECIDE

Ϙ TOP TIP

"Great minds discuss ideas;
Average minds discuss events;
Small minds discuss people."

— **Eleanor Roosevelt**

CHAPTER 12
LAYOUT, STRUCTURE AND WEIGHT

REASON 9:
YOU DIDN'T HAVE A CLEAR AND LOGICAL STRUCTURE. YOU DIDN'T GIVE THE RIGHT AMOUNT OF WEIGHT TO EACH ISSUE.

If you don't plan, there is a real risk that your arguments get mixed up together. A confusing opinion with arguments not set out in an easy to follow structure will not get high marks. A confusing structure will mean that all the good work you have done in preparing, reading, thinking and evaluating will not be obvious to the examiner. You are wasting valuable marks.

Equally bad as an unclear structure is the failure to give sufficient significance and weight to each point. This means you spent too much time on points that were straight-forward and not enough time and detail on points that were important or complicated.

The Solutions:
STEP 9: Adopt a clear and logical structure. Give the right amount of weight to each issue.

Why do I need to plan a structure for my opinion

Think of the structure of your opinion as the frame that will support all the content you will put in your opinion. A good structure is going to help make your opinion easy to read and stand out from other opinions. All good opinions have a good structure that shows off their content. Why do all mammals have a backbone? So they can stand out and be seen!

THE GENERAL OPINION STRUCTURE (the main frame)

The structure of an opinion is formed in two areas. First there is the **general overall structure of the opinion, the main frame. This includes all the main headings and sub-heading for an opinion on that subject.** For example, the introduction, background, summary of facts, the main legal headings (which depend on your subject), evidence, procedural matters and next steps. Think of this as a tent, the outside canvas and main frame of the tent. Different subjects have different overall structures; different main frames. An opinion on contract law will have a different structure from an opinion dealing with breach of statutory law or negligence.

The second area you need to structure into your opinion is the order of the content. **The main factual and legal arguments will need their own structure; this is where you decide how you will structure the content of your opinion.** In our tent example, this shows how you organise the inside of your tent. In a breach of contract dispute, this would be how you decided to order the different allegations of breach within that section. **This is the content structure.**

Since there are different structures for different opinions, you must think about your opinion structure in the planning stage and never simply apply the same structure to every opinion. Each opinion is different from the previous one and the structure you choose will change depending on the issues and the subject.

You will be provided with sample written opinions/ structures by your University or College. Don't ignore them. Build up a precedent folder and find general structures that you can use as a starting point for similar opinions, on the same areas of law. You start with your general structure and then adapt and modify it for each new opinion to fit the facts and issues.

There are a few general points that can be made about the general overall opinion structure (the main frame):

Introduction
Most opinions start by confirming the party you are instructed to act for and summarising what you have been asked to consider in your instructions.

Background
No opinion should start by discussing the main factual or legal arguments. The background introduces the key facts and the context of the discussion. This section sets the scene for the discussion that will follow.

Preliminary issues
A preliminary issue is any problems you need to tackle before you get into the main factual or legal discussion. This section

may define key words, could include an interpretation of an important issue, statutory terms or evidence. If you find you have no preliminary points, then ignore this section and move to the next section.

Summary of Advice

This will have a concise summary of the main points you have been asked to advise on. Make sure you deal with ALL points. I cannot tell you the times I read assessment opinions where students dealt with all matters in the body of the opinion but failed to record the key points in their summary of advice. For example, you are asked to advise on liability and quantum in a negligence claim. You deal with liability, contributory negligence and quantum in the body of the opinion. There should be a concise summary on each of these three issues in the summary of advice. Many solicitors start reading counsel's written opinion by turning to the summary of advice and reading this first!

Conclusion

Your final conclusion may be in the form of a summary of advice or in a section headed conclusion. This will depend on the format your university or college recommends you use.

Your arguments or discussion in the main body of the opinion should be consistent with the arguments and evaluations you have made earlier in your opinion. The final conclusion should not be a surprise.

Evidence/ Next Steps

Every opinion should provide practical advice on these areas unless your instructions make it clear that you are NOT required to cover this area. Remember the purpose of most opinions is for your instructing solicitors and client to work out what to do next. Your advice in this area needs to be adjusted to fit your instructions, the current procedural position of the claim and the requirements of the Civil Procedural Rules and Practice Directions. Remember that you also need to advise on any ethical issues arising from your instructions or case papers.

CONTENT STRUCTURE (the internal arrangement)

The main factual and legal arguments will need their own structure; this is where you decide how you will structure the content of your opinion. Your R.E.D. learning strategy put your arguments in order, starting with the best argument on top and then working down toward arguments with less merit. You may choose this as the content structure for your opinion; we will call this **best argument on top structure**.

Another structure is to discuss arguments in the order they arise, we call this in **chronological order**. You start at the beginning or earliest event and work forward to the current time or last event. You may also use a structure where you discuss arguments by grouping them together into topics in an order that you decide, a **topic structure**.

Sometimes the opinion question will suggest a content structure for you, let's call this follow the question structure. For example, if you are asked to discuss three issues in a particular order that should be the structure for your opinion. When you deal with each point in the order they arise in your instructions, we call this **follow the question structure**.

Sometimes the subject may suggest an obvious content structure to tackle the opinion. I call this the **subject structure**. Imagine you must discuss a biological process, such as the production and development of blood cells in the human body. The logical place to start is at the beginning of the process by describing the component part of blood, how is it produced and what it does in the human body. You may then move on to discuss the system for transporting blood and how blood cells are damaged and then repaired by the human body. **In the planning stage consider at least two potential content structures. Ask yourself which structure is the easiest for the examiner to follow?**

> ➢ best argument on top?
> ➢ chronological order?
> ➢ topic order?
> ➢ follow the opinion question?
> ➢ follow the subject?

WHERE DO YOU PUT YOUR VIEWS IN AN OPINION STRUCTURE

OK, having considered the different types of opinion structures (the main frame and content structures) what have you missed out? Your interpretation and assessment of the issues? **You must plan where to put YOUR ideas for each new opinion.** You cannot simply put them in the same place every time. You need to **choose a place that works with your opinion structure, content structure, instructions and HELPS THE READER.** The end of each key issue or the end of the opinion are usually the best place to put Your ideas.

There are several places to consider putting your ideas:

Beginning of Each Issue

What about putting your ideas after you discuss factual and legal issues but before you refer to any judgment or other authorities? This is probably NOT a great place as it is far too early and your examiner will expect you to discuss the issue, any judgments, judicial guidance, procedural guidance or interpretations from law text books before you comment.

End of Each Issue

If you are using the topic structure, it may be a good idea to put your views at the end of each topic after you have discussed the views or interpretations in any judgments or other authorities. If you have several topics, then at the end of each topic, where you wish to express an alternative view or opinion, may be a good place rather than leaving all your ideas until the very end of the opinion.

End of the Opinion

Some students prefer to put their ideas at the very end of the opinion just before the final conclusion. This structure can work well especially if your opinion is about predicting or commenting on future developments. Placing your ideas about future developments towards the end of the opinion fits into a chronological structure.

The important task is to spend time thinking about where you are going to put YOUR views and mark it out on your opinion plan.

WEIGHTING YOUR OPINION

The last but important decision is deciding where you put the most detail in your opinion. The general rule is that the more important, complex or central to your main discussion the more detail and therefore the more time you should spend writing about these problems. These topics will also occupy the most space in your opinion. The reverse of this problem is too much detail dealing with issues that are not complicated or in dispute between the parties. If an issue is NOT complicated or contentious make your point and move on; don't spend lots of time writing about it.

I often had to read assessment opinions where students clearly had not thought about how they were going to weight their opinion. They wrote too much detail on introductory or background issues and very little on the real problems they needed to address. These opinions would have pages and pages of background information, some students simply wrote out the large sections of their instructions or witness statements and then they wrote very little about the disputed issues because they could not evaluate the evidence or had not properly planned their opinion. These opinions didn't get valuable marks because they simply didn't have enough detail in the right places in their opinions. Students don't get marks for just writing lengthy opinions otherwise everyone who handed in their eight-page opinion would get a great grade. **Students obtain outstanding grades for correctly advising on the right factual and legal issues with the appropriate amount of detail in the right parts of their opinion.**

Opinions With Word Limits

If your examiner, university or college, set a word limit for opinions, you should avoid going over the limit as there are usually penalties for doing this. You will find this information in your assessment or assignment instructions. You will want to maximize your opinion marks so you should NOT write an opinion that is significantly less than your word limit. For example, if you are asked to write an opinion not exceeding 3,000 words or 10 pages you should NOT write an opinion of 1,000 words or 2 pages. The chances are you have missed out some important issues.

Having done your legal research and written your opinion don't try to write more just to get within the word limit. All you will do is repeat what you have already said and this will not get you extra marks. For example, if you have a 3,000-word limit, you have written 2,700 words and have fully advised on all issues - stop writing!

AN OVERVIEW ON PLANNING, STRUCTURE AND WEIGHTING

You must decide and plan where the most important and complex issues are in your opinion. Make sure that you give these complex or important areas the most detail and space in your opinion. This will mean that you take the reader to the core of your arguments and spend the most time at the right places. **Examiners are more inclined to mark work highly when it has been well planned, structured and has the right amount of detail in the right areas, so plan it out before writing your opinion.**

SEVEN important questions you should ask when recording your **opinion plan**:

1. **What general structure (main frame) should I use for my opinion?**

2. **What should I put in the background section?**

3. Do I have any **preliminary issues** that I need to deal with first?

4. **What structure should I use for my content (content structure)?**

> ➢ best argument on top?
>
> ➢ chronological order?
>
> ➢ topic order?
>
> ➢ follow the opinion question structure?
>
> ➢ follow the subject structure?

5. **Where will I put MY own views** in this opinion?

6. **Where will I spend more time writing (weighting)**?

7. What are my **conclusions?** (on each main issue and a final conclusion)

READ. EVALUATE. DECIDE

ᴄᶐ TOP TIP

Preparation, Preparation, Preparation

"You're off to Great Places!" [8]

---

[8] Dr Seuss Oh, The Places You'll Go

CHAPTER 13
HOW TO WRITE AN OUTSTANDING OPINION

REASON 10:
YOU DIDN'T WRITE YOUR OPINION IN A LANGUAGE AND STYLE APPROPRIATE FOR A PROFESSIONAL OPINION.

The Solution:
STEP 10: Write your opinion in a language and style appropriate for a professional opinion.

A clear logical structure is the best way of showing off the great reading, thinking and evaluating you have already done. If you can also write your opinion in a style that is easy to read your work should get great scores.

Writing an outstanding opinion starts with clearly communicating with the examiner. Your writing style is the way you communicate your ideas, arguments, interpretation and opinions. To communicate your message clearly it is important that your work is easy to read. When you say what you mean, keep it simple and write in a formal style - the job is done.

SAY WHAT YOU MEAN & KEEP IT SIMPLE

The most important thing to remember is that you should write clearly so your meaning is easy to understand. Avoid writing anything that is confusing, vague, unclear, conflicts with earlier views or simply fails to communicate what you mean. **The easiest way of being understood is to just say what you mean and keep it simple.**

Saying what you mean and keeping it simple means finding the **balance between not being too brief (and leaving out the details) and writing too much so you write about irrelevant information. You need to discuss the key issues and set out the arguments in your opinion but in a way that does not become repetitive, rambling or difficult to follow for the reader.** When you over-use language the words get in the way of your arguments and distracts the examiner from focusing on the important information. Too much irrelevant information is frustrating because it hides the important information. Do you have friends who just can't get to the point in a conversation? How hard and frustrating is it when you just want to know the point of the very long story? **An advantage of saying what you mean and keeping it simple is that it will keep you on topic.**

HOW TO FIND THE RIGHT WRITING STYLE FOR AN OPINION

Even when you understand the core rule of saying what you mean and keeping it simple you ALSO must remember to WRITE IN A STYLE APPROPRIATE FOR AN OPINION. **Try to think of your writing style as the way you would speak to a**

person if you were having a conversation.

Informal Writing[9]

Think of the sort of language you would use if you were texting a friend, it would be informal. The sentences may be incomplete. You may use abbreviations or words that have a special meaning between friends rather than their literal meaning. Your style may communicate your personality or feelings by using smiley faces, emoji or other icons. You may include jokes and punctuations that reflect your mood such as capital letters or exclamation marks.

Informal writing is NEVER acceptable in opinions. You must try very hard not to slip into this style of writing. Would you write to your friends in the same style you would write to your boss or manager at work? No!

Formal Writing

Opinions require a formal style of writing. Think of the style of reports and books written by professors, lawyers, experts, academics and published authors. You need to write your opinion in a formal style of writing. **Think of your writing style as a reflection of how you speak to another professional - so it is time to put on your best voice!** Your best voice does not mean a pompous voice with lots of unnecessary old-fashioned words. Think of this voice as a **modern, polite and professional voice**.

You should write in complete sentences. You should choose the correct words and terminology for your subject. You should use standard grammar and the correct spelling for words in the UK.

---

[9] I have written this book in informal language because I want you to relax and concentrate on reading this book; you will have plenty of formal books to read on your course.

Let's recap:

- ✓ Say what you mean
- ✓ Keep it simple
- ✓ Write in a formal style

◖ TOP TIP

Either write something worth reading or do something worth writing."

— **Benjamin Franklin**

Follow the Rules – Grammar and Spelling

Your final challenge is to make sure that you follow the basic rules of grammar and spelling because this will allow your examiner to understand the meaning of your words quickly. Poor punctuation, grammar and spelling requires your examiner to re-read your work to understand its intended meaning. The more the examiner has to stop and re-read the more distracted they are from your legal advice in your opinion.

Imagine you are having a conversation with a friend. You are opposite each other and she/he is telling you something serious that you need to hear. Behind your friend and in your eyesight is someone jumping up and down and waving at you. You are trying to listen to your friend but the person behind her/him is distracting you. Poor grammar just gets in the way of reading the interesting content you are writing; this is why it is important to spend time getting the grammar and spelling right.

You should always use a dictionary or a grammar reference book to check the rules. When you are unsure don't just guess. The rules of grammar and spelling are not always logical! Have a look at appendix C for recommended reference books and websites.

Get the Grammar Right

A short recap of some basic rules of grammar.

> **The sentence.**
> A sentence always starts with a capital letter and usually ends with a full stop. There must be a subject noun, a person or thing, which is the focus of the sentence. There must be a verb which is a word that expresses action or an occurrence. There must be an object of the

sentence, to whom or to which the action is done.

e.g. James grabbed the child to stop her running in front of the car.

In this example 'James' is the subject noun, the action 'grabbed' is the verb and "the child" is the object noun. Sentences are the essential building blocks for your writing. Sentences can vary in length. There are short and long sentences. The rules on constructing sentences become more complicated the longer the sentence. **If you are not familiar with advanced rules of grammar just say what you mean and keep it short**. If your sentence ends with a question, always end the sentence with a question mark (?).

➢ **Paragraphs–**
These are groups of sentences on the same topic or issue. Paragraphs help the reader to break up the text into topics that they can read more easily and quickly. The key rule is that **one issue = one paragraph**.

Generally, a paragraph should NOT consist of one sentence. If you find one sentence on its own in a paragraph, ask whether it belongs to the previous or next paragraph.

Long paragraphs are more difficult to read than shorter paragraphs. When checking your work look for very long paragraphs. Ask: have I dealt with more than one issue in this paragraph? If you have dealt with more than one issue break the paragraph where you start to deal with the new issue.

Long paragraphs are more difficult to read than shorter paragraphs. It is easier to read paragraphs of varying sizes rather than paragraphs that are all the same length. Vary the size of your paragraphs if you find they are all the same length by adding a bit more or taking out something irrelevant. When checking your work look for very long paragraphs and break them up. You should never have a paragraph that is the whole length of a page. A paragraph size will depend on your topic and will generally be about four or five sentences.

➢ **Commas [,]**
These little symbols help to punctuate sentences. They help to separate the main part of the sentence from a sub-clause (a part of the sentence). Never use a comma before the word 'and'.

Example
'the blue car shot past the driver, despite his best efforts to avoid it, and hit his car.'

The main sentence is 'the blue car shot past the driver and hit his car; the sub-clause is 'despite his best efforts to avoid it.'

Commas also separate qualifying words.

Example
'However, despite a great goal, the goal-keeper performed very well.'

Commas are also used to separate items in a list.

Example
'Despite the collision, the driver did well to maintain control of his car.'
Here the qualifying clause is "despite the collision" and the main clause of the sentence is that "...the driver did well to maintain control of his car."

Commas are also used to separate items in a list (but don't use it to separate the last item).

Example
"You should read, evaluate, decide, plan and then write an outstanding opinion."

> **Quotation marks ['...']**
You may want to quote a short extract from a judgment or from a witness statement in your opinion. Short quotations of words spoken or written by a person of one or two sentences can be incorporated into a sentence using quotations marks at the beginning and end of the quotation.   A quotation of spoken or written words of MORE than two sentences should start on a new line after a colon [:] or be preceded with a comma.

Example
Hayley wrote in her diary:
"I will never forget the face of that driver, on that summer day in 2016 when my life changed forever. He was a reckless idiot."
If you are not quoting a complete sentence or only part of a quotation, then you should introduce the quotation with **three** leader dots [...]. The leader dots start where you shorten the section from the quotation. Leader dots

may appear at the beginning, in the middle or at the end of a sentence. Where the leader dots are removed will depend on which parts of the quotation you wish to focus the reader's attention on. In the examples below you will see this demonstrated.

Example

Extract from Sarjit's witness statement
"I saw a woman take £50 from her hand bag and hand it to a young man. He looked like her son. He smiled at the woman and walked off."

- The witness stated, "I saw the woman take £50 from her hand bag…"

- The witness stated he saw, "…a young man. He looked like her son. He smiled at the woman and walked off."

- The witness stated, "I saw the woman take £50 from her hand bag and hand it to a young man…"

➢ Take a careful note
The key to using quotations properly is accurate record taking. You need to devise a system where you indicate in your record or notes:

- the author

- publication or document (including year and edition for publications)

- reference page

- make sure you record quotations accurately.

➢ **Semi-colon [;]**
The semi-colon joins two parts of a sentence that could be linked or separated with a full stop. They occur where one part of a sentence immediately follows on to the second part.

Example
Harry was annoyed with P J; he had been rude and offensive to his friend, Monica.
The same sentence could be written as two short sentences.
Harry was annoyed with PJ. He had been rude and offensive to his friend, Monica.

Here using either format for your sentence(s) would be correct. You choose which format you prefer. You must however apply the correct punctuation to the sentence structure you choose.

➢ **Colon [:]**
A colon is used to set up a quotation, to introduce a list of items or to define or expand a statement.

Example

- PC Jones collected the victim's things: her shoes, bag, winter scarf, hat and coat.

SPELLING - GET IT RIGHT

Examiners hate reading poor spelling because it slows down their reading and understanding of the work. Poor spelling means the examiner must spend time guessing what the word should be or re-reading the work to try and understand the intended meaning.

There are two main reasons why students have spelling errors in their work. **Some students do not read the final version of their work** and therefore do not spot the errors in spelling and grammar they know how to fix but just don't read. This is easy to fix – READ your final opinion BEFORE you submit it for marking. I know that sometime deadlines are tight but having done all that good work it seems such a waste of easy marks not to make sure your work is presented at its best. Find a quiet café, park or somewhere in the library on a comfortable chair and read your work carefully without distractions.

The second reason for spelling and grammar errors is where students use a correctly spelt word but in the wrong context; this is when you need help with a grammar reference book or dictionary. Sometimes the correct spelling of a word depends on the meaning and context of the sentence. Common examples where the spell checker will not help you are with the words: lose/loose, your/ you're, their/there. Use a grammar reference book or a dictionary to help you get grammar and spelling right. Have a look at Appendix C for my recommended reference resources.

Always apply a spell checker to your final work and then YOU need to check it for mistakes.

- ➤ Check for missing words that have not been added to the sentence.
- ➤ Find words that for some freaky reason the spell checker did not find.
- ➤ Spot those words that the auto-correcting or predictive text spelling function on your laptop changed to a word you did not want to use.
- ➤ Check to see if words have more than one way of spelling them. There is often a difference between spelling the same words in the USA and UK.

Remember names and laces will not always be found by a spell checker. Did you spot the spelling error in the last sentence? laces instead of places!

Best Time for Checking

I find that the best time to check my work is in the morning when my mind is fresh. Try to write your opinion and then leave it for at least 24 hours, the longer the better.

Your mind needs the time to forget what you thought you wrote and to see what you have actually written.

The worst time to check your work is when you are under pressure from a deadline or tired. Too many students check their opinions as they stand in line to hand in their assessment opinions and it looks perfect until they get their grade.

READY TO COMPLETE THAT OPINION

When planning and writing your opinion you will:

- ✓ Apply **R.E.D.- Read. Evaluate. Decide.**
- ✓ **Plan** your structure.
- ✓ Spend more time on the important main topics or problems (**weighting**).
- ✓ **Write - say what you mean & keep it simple.**
- ✓ Write – **stay on topic.**
- ✓ Write in a **formal style.**
- ✓ **Check** your grammar and spelling.

℺ TOP TIP

"A good head and good heart are always a formidable combination. But when you add to that a literate tongue or pen, then you have something very special."

— Nelson Mandela

CHAPTER 14
FORMAL ASSESSMENTS & PLAGIARISM

W HEN STUDENTS HAVE NOT BEEN CAREFUL in recording the source of information in their reading material they cannot identify where information came from or separate their own thoughts from published sources. When you get confused it is easy to accidently use someone else's words as if they were your own.

PLAGIARISM IS SERIOUS ACADEMIC MISCONDUCT

The Bar Standard Board, universities and colleges have very strict policies on plagiarism and consider it serious misconduct. Universities and colleges have computer software that can process assessment opinions and record the percentage of material in your opinion that corresponds with published material; you will NOT fool your college or university.

Students fail to realise that published works have a style of writing that is very easy to spot and very different from the way most students write. Students often cut and paste extracts from published works into their notes because it is easier than writing out the note; this is ok. You must NOT however just cut and paste that work into your opinion WITHOUT referring to the original author. When I assessed opinions I sometimes read papers where parts were taken from published sources but had not been properly referenced. There was a clear difference between the published author and the student's own writing style.

HOW DO YOU USE SAMPLE OPINIONS IN AN OPEN BOOK ASSESSMENT

Sample opinions are guides for you to use in assessments but you must understand how to use them. **The sample opinions provide a guide to demonstrate the skill of opinion writing**. Can you just cut and paste parts of the sample answers into your assessment opinion and pretend you have written it? No. If you want to gain marks you must write the opinion in your own words. You may cite the same law and cases but your interpretation, evaluation and application to the facts must be YOUR own work. **Use a sample opinion as a guide, don't just copy and paste large parts into your assessment opinion if you want to get those outstanding grades.**

Assessment Opinions Need to Be Your Own Work

The assessment rules require that the work you submit is ALL your own work. You cannot discuss or collaborate with other students in preparing and writing your ASSESSMENT opinions. Make sure that you do not discuss or share your work with other students.

When students work together they will use similar words, phrases or even make the same errors in the same places in their opinions. These are all signs that you have worked or collaborated with other students, so do not be tempted.

A final word of warning: sometimes when students are desperate they take or copy another student's opinion and hand it in as their own work. Make sure you never leave your computer without logging out a password protected screen. Don't send your work to printers that you have not tested are working; you don't want your work printing out several days later for other students to pick up. Make sure when you send your opinion to print you are at the printer to collect ALL your printed copies before someone else takes them.

Never share your storage device or allow other students to access your cloud or folders with assessment opinions. Always keep draft copies of your work until final examinations results are formally announced. If there is a dispute you can prove that you wrote that outstanding opinion.

SHOULD I GET AN OPINION WRITING COMPANY TO WRITE MY OPINION

There are commercial companies that can provide you with a suggested opinion plan and opinion answer for your assessment. You will be in breach of the BSB and your university's assessment rules if you submit work that is not entirely your own work.

Do not be tempted to take this short cut. These opinions will not help you when you need to sit in an examination room on your own with an assessment paper. There are no short cuts to organising your thoughts, learning how to read, evaluate and decide what you think and finally writing an outstanding opinion. **What you learn each time you write an opinion is an investment in your future that will develop your future learning, as opposed to a one-off opinion purchase.**

¶ TOP TIP

"Don't settle for less than you can be."

— **Jim Rohn, American entrepreneur, author and motivational speaker.**

CHAPTER 15
CONCLUSION

"Be the change that you wish to see in the world."

— MAHATMA GANDHI

T HE PURPOSE OF THIS BOOK is to help you understand how to write an outstanding opinion and to provide you with tools to improve your opinion writing skill. Follow the advice in this book and you should find the skill to plan, organise and write opinions that fulfil the criteria for the BPTC assessments. You have to put in the hard work with your legal research and understanding the substantive law and procedural rules.

When you start using R.E.D. learning you will get quicker and better at applying these simple steps. You will spend MORE time thinking and evaluating. You will find YOUR own views. When you have completed your first opinion using R.E.D. learning, I hope you will feel great – CONGRATULATIONS!

Your opinions are the way you will show that you have:

- **understood** your legal subjects
- the **skills** to critically assess information

- the **ability** to present information in a format that is intelligent, logical and persuasive
- the **intelligence** and skills for independent thinking
- the **skills** to write a professional legal opinion.

Remember at the start of the book we looked at the ten reasons you didn't write an outstanding opinion; now it is time to review your progress.

10 REASONS
YOU WROTE
AN OUTSTANDING OPINION

1. You **read** your instructions and case papers **properly**.

2. You **identified the** key or **important facts**.

3. You **identified ALL** the key factual and legal **problems**.

4. You **understood the arguments**.

5. You **think** like a barrister.

6. You **evaluated** the law, facts, evidence and issues.

7. You got the **right answers** and **expressed an opinion** on key issues.

8. You set out your **reasoning and conclusions**.

9. You had a **clear and logical structure**. You gave the right amount of **weight** to each issue.

10. You wrote your opinion in a **language and style** appropriate for a professional opinion.

CONGRATULATIONS

Your legal opinions are the way that you will start your journey towards your legal career. Dream it, Plan it, Do it, can you see your future? The right study skills will help you to achieve your full potential.

Study skills for students is the first part of your development. As you embark on a professional career you will develop work and life skills to take you to further dreams.

People have over thousands of years used their skills to thrive, develop and adapt. Your study, work and life skills are the culmination of human development over millions of years. I wish you an epic journey into that future and leave you with the words of an amazing human being, Mr. Nelson Mandela:

"Education is the most powerful weapon you can use to change the world."

– NELSON MANDELA

Remember to download your FREE OPINION PLANNING infographics. If you intend to continue to masters' level or beyond, my next book, *7 Mistakes Students Don't make in 1ˢᵗ Class Dissertations*, will help you plan and write your next dissertation; it will be published in 2017. Sign up to be notified of publication date on www.inspiredtostudy.org

APPENDICES

Appendix A – 5 Stages of Opinion Writing

Appendix B – How to Work Out Time Estimates

Appendix C – Recommended further reading for grammar and
spelling

Appendix D – The key to good preparation -
sleep, eat, exercise and relax.

APPENDIX A - 5 STAGES OF OPINION WRITING

THE 5 STAGES OF OPINION WRITING	
STAGE 1	Start by **reading** your instructions and outline case papers
STAGE 2	main legal research and detailed reading of your case papers
STAGE 3	Thinking and planning
STAGE 4	writing your opinion
STAGE 5	check that opinion

Stage 1: Read your instructions

You should read your opinion instructions, background information and any diagrams, maps or timelines you have been provided. Read the information about the deadline for submission (record the time and date carefully) and any rules or guidance for completing the task. Read the case papers so you understand the broad issues and legal area of study you will need to research. Think of this first stage as a warm up session.

Stage 2: Main research and detail reading

This is the time for your legal research and detailed reading of your case papers. Your research and reading will form the main content of your opinion. This is complex reading that will take the longest time and requires the most focus. This is when you are so engrossed in reading you should forget all about your phone, social media or texting your friends. No distractions are allowed.

Stage 3: Thinking and planning

There is no point in research and reading if you do not have time to think about what you have read and plan what you are going to write. At this stage you should complete an opinion plan.

Stage 4: Writing your opinion

The time this takes will depend on how quickly you type or write, the length of opinion and how well you have planned at stage three. At this stage don't include time for editing, checking or minor structural changes to your opinion.

Stage 5: Time to check your work

This is the time to check your opinion, edit and carry out any minor structural changes. Run the spell checker AND re-read the opinion for spelling and grammar errors not picked up by the spell checker. No work is complete until it has been properly checked twice!

Remember visit **www.inspiredtostudy.org** to download your FREE OPINION PLANNING infographics.

APPENDIX B – HOW TO WORK OUT A TIME ESTIMATE

GUESS the time you need to:

Stage 1. - Read the introductory materials, your instructions and an outline of the case papers.

Stage 2. - Carry out your main research and detailed reading of the case papers.

Stage 3. - Thinking and planning.

Stage 4. - Writing your opinion.

Stage 5. - Checking your opinion.

REMEMBER you need to have time for BREAKS, LUNCH AND DINNER so add in periods for your breaks at stages that YOU find convenient.

ADD UP YOUR TIME

Time to add up the time you have estimated for stages 1 - 5 if you intend to complete the work in one go. If you intend to check your work later then add up the time for the tasks under stages 1 - 4.

You will get better at judging the time for the five stages the more you use this system. It is important that you **make sure you have the time to complete the work you have planned** or re-think your schedule. You can break up the time to fit each stage if you plan your work over several days as long as they are kept in the same order.

SET YOUR TIMER & BEGIN

Set a timer on your watch, phone or PC for the time you have allowed for stage one. Now put the timer out of sight and start to complete the work. When the timer goes off have you completed the task? If you have not completed the task guess how much longer you need, re-set the timer and put it out of sight and return to your work. Once you have completed stage one, set the timer for stage two and move on until you get to stage five.

EXAMPLE of a TIME ESTIMATE PLAN for 1 day

Stage	Task	Time estimate
1	Reading instructions	15 mins
2	Research and detail reading	180 min
	(Break for lunch)	
3	Thinking and planning	45 mins
	(Break for coffee)	
4	Writing	60 mins
	(Break for tea and cakes)	
5	Checking	30 mins
	Total time	330 mins (5 hours 30 mins)

REMEMBER:

1. You need to add in break times, they often fit in at the end of one of the stages or after about 30-45 minutes of study. Having regular and short rest breaks is key to keeping your mind alert and thinking logically. It is not a good idea to sit at your desk for hours or to try and complete the whole process whilst you are tired, see appendix D.

2. You can complete your work over several days. Try to finish a stage before taking a break for a day or more. You will find that when you start the new stage the following day(s) later you will need to re-read your earlier work to just to get up to speed with your previous thoughts and work.

EXAMPLE of a TIME ESTIMATE PLAN over 3 days

Stage	Task	Time estimate
1	Reading instructions	15 mins
2	Research and reading	180 min
	(Include a couple of mini breaks)	
Day 1		**3 hours 15 mins**
3	Thinking and planning	45 mins
Day 2		**45 mins**
4	Writing	60 mins
	(Break for tea)	
5	Checking	30 mins
Day 3		**90 mins**
3 days	**Total time**	**5 hours 30 mins**

EXAMPLE of a TIME ESTIMATE PLAN for an assessment

for 3 hours & 30 minutes

You will have already:

- carried out your legal research on the core law
- **collected sample precedent opinions** provided by your university or college
- collected **sample general structure** for different types of opinions
- You may have prepared your own blank generic opinion plan

Time plan	Stage	Task	Time estimate	% of time
09.00	1	Reading instructions & case papers	45 mins	21%
09.45	2	Research[10]	15 min	7.5%
10.00	3	Thinking and planning[11]	45 mins	21%
10.45	4	Writing	90 mins	43%
12.15	5	Checking	15 mins	7.5%
		Total time	**3 hours 30 mins**	**100%**

---

[10] Research in this context is just organising your earlier research papers and locating the correct statutes, regulations and cases relevant to the facts in the assessment paper.
[11] Note you are NOT writing your opinion for at least 1hour after the beginning of the assessment – this is RED time. You are reading, evaluating and deciding on key issues.

- Remember in assessments conditions you need to **pay attention to the time - it progresses really fast!** There is no point in outstanding reading, evaluation and decisions if you do not leave sufficient time to WRITE and CHECK your opinion.

- **Practice at least one timed opinion** under assessment conditions **BEFORE the final assessment** this will help you work out YOUR Time Plan and help you manage your time in the real assessment.

- **Have a Time Plan** that works for YOU – record the actual time you need to start the key stages and have it in front of you. The plan above assumes the assessment starts at 09.00 and finishes at 13.30. As you hit your time markers finish your stage quickly if you have not done so and move on to the next section so you stay on track.

- Remember you cannot use a timer or device that makes a sound during the assessment.

Visit **www.inspiredtostudy.org** to download your FREE OPINION PLANNING infographics.

APPENDIX C- RECOMMENDED READING FOR GRAMMAR AND SPELLING

Dictionary

Little Oxford English Dictionary, University Press or online at

http://www.oxforddictionaries.com/definition/english/online

http://www.collinsdictionary.com/english-thesaurus

Grammar reference

http://learnenglish.britishcouncil.org/en/quick-grammar

http://www.bbc.co.uk/skillswise/topic-group/sentence-grammar

Reference

Oxford Thesaurus of English, University Press or online at

http://www.oxforddictionaries.com/thesaurus/

Visit **www.inspiredtostudy.org** to download your FREE in-fographics.

APPENDIX D – THE KEY TO GOOD PREPARATION — SLEEP. EAT. EXERCISE. RELAX.

"To keep the body in good health is a duty ...otherwise we shall not be able to keep our mind strong and clear."

– BUDDHA

There is no point spending hours sitting at a desk if you are not ready or able to study. It is essential that you understand that being healthy is a part of your preparation for effective study. If you are tired, ill or have poor concentration your study will NOT be effective.

The solutions - four simple steps:

SLEEP

EAT

EXERCISE

RELAX

The 'I don't have time' excuse

You don't have time to eat, sleep, exercise or relax because you have an opinion to write. Your whole ability to think logically is dependent on four simple steps. When you are tired and stressed you produce your worst work because your thinking is not clear or logical. Your ability to judge the quality of your work is badly affected by a lack of sleep, lack of exercise, stress and a persistently poor diet.

The power of sleep

Have you heard of the phrase 'I want to sleep on it'? It generally means someone wants more time to think about a decision, usually overnight while they sleep on the problem. Research has shown that whilst sleeping the mind can find solutions and connections that the conscious mind could not make whilst awake[12]. Your ability to form arguments, make connections and find solutions to those tough opinion questions could be improved by a good night's sleep.

EAT

You cannot study properly whilst you are hungry, so eat well. You need to keep hydrated so also drink plenty of water. This is not the time to be skipping meals or forgetting to drink during the day. You need energy and water to think and write well. If the brain does not have to worry about food and water it will be ready and able to focus on writing that opinion.

Do you want some help with easy to follow healthy food recipes? Go to Snig's Kitchen for a celebration of food from around the world, recipes, cooking tips and reviews

http://snigskitchen.blogspot.co.uk/

---

[12] Nature 2004 Jan 22, Sleep Inspires insight, by Wagner U, Gais S, Haider H, Verleger R and Born J

Exercise

You cannot spend all your time at your desk. There are serious health consequences of spending too much time sitting at a desk.[13] Researchers recommend breaking up sitting after 30 minutes with one to two minutes of short activity. Have a look at the recommended fitness guidelines for activity and try some of the fitness tests.[14]

---

[13] www.nhs.uk/livewell/fitness. These range from the risks associated with obesity, diabetes, cardiovascular events and some forms of cancer.

[14] http://www.nhs.uk/livewell/fitness - See for recommended activity. Try the online fitness test.

Recent Research

Recent research from Stanford University found that walking helped to boost the creative thinking of people undergoing testing compared with those who were seated during the test period. For those in the test, walking outside had even better test results. The research concluded: "Walking opens up the free flow of ideas, and it is a simple and robust solution to the goals of increasing creativity and increasing physical activity."[15] Have a break between classes and lectures, go to the gym, go for a walk with friends or just get some fresh air.

Relax

We all have periods when stressful events happen, that is life. Find your true friends and share your concerns. Try to find a long-term fix for the problem. If the problem is too big for you to fix, talk to someone you trust. This could be a professional such as a doctor, counsellor, parent, someone from your religious community or a teacher. Just talking about a problem helps to relieve stress so imagine how good it would be to get some helpful advice and solve the problem?

All colleges and universities have teachers and counsellors who are committed to helping you with any personal problems so reach out and get that help. There are wellbeing classes and courses that help you find coping strategies when you feel stressed and help you understand the factors that trigger stress.

Remember relaxing also means having fun, so go out and enjoy yourself with friends and family. Some students think they cannot take time out to enjoy themselves especially near to assessments. This is the very time you need to relax and

---

[15] Oppezzo, Marily; Schwartz, Daniel L. Journal of Experimental Psychology: Learning, Memory, and Cognition, Vol 40(4), Jul 2014, 1142-1152. (Oppezzo & L, 2014 July)

have fun so take an evening off and do something you enjoy.
When you return to your revision you will feel refreshed, ready
to focus and think like a barrister.

BIBLIOGRAPHY

Retrieved from Oxforddictionaries.com: http://www.ox-forddictionaries.com (January 2016)

Department of Health. (2004). *At least five a week*. London.

Fry Ketteridge and Marshall. (2003). *A Handbook for Teaching and Learning in Higher Education*. London: Kogan Page.

NHS direct. (2015, July 11). NHS.uk. Retrieved from http://www.nhs.uk/Livewell/fitness/Pages/physical-activity-guidelines-for-adults.aspx.

Oppezzo, M., & L, S. D. (2014 July). Learning, Memory and Cognition. *Journal of Experimental Psychology vol 40* (4), 1142-1152.

Seuss, D. (2003). *Oh, The Places You'll Go!* London: HarperCollinsChildren's Book.

Stevenson. (2002). Little Oxford English Dictionary. Oxford: Oxford University Press.

About the Author

Suzanne Reece is an education coach. She is a solicitor (currently non-practising) who worked in legal firms for over 17 years. She later moved into education teaching post graduate law at City, University of London for nearly 10 years. Critical to her role were skills teaching, course design and assessments. Suzanne also supervised LLM dissertation students, delivered academic support and provided study coaching to post -graduates students.

Early in her education career it became apparent that good students were not achieving the grades they deserved. Suzanne discovered that for some students their poor study skills prevented their academic knowledge being communicated to their tutors in the right form. With the right study skills Suzanne believes that students can remove these obstacles and achieve their full potential. Her passion is helping students achieve first class grades.

Suzanne has taught thousands of students and helped them obtain first class grades. In 2015, she established Inspired to Study Ltd to provide bespoke educational skills training. Suzanne provides personal coaching and mentoring. She runs regular webinars, workshops and attends speaking events. To find our more visit, www.inspiredtostudy.org

Suzanne Reece
The Study Coach
Education Coach, Lecturer & Author

www.inspiredtostudy.org

ACKNOWLEDGEMENTS

Special thanks to my brother and sister, Arlon and Deborah Reece, for their love.

To Deborah, Gillian, Lesley and Sian for their impressive work in carefully editing this book. To Hayley for her careful checking. To Paul for his kind words in the Foreword.

To all those who gave helpful suggestions, support and encouragement: Paul Brooks, Hayley Brown, Paula Edwards, George Georgiou, Shirley Harper, Lesley Hicks, Sian Lewis, Ian Martin, Deborah Reece, Hazel Rosemin, Marcia Scott, Surinder Tamne, Gillian Woodworth. Special thanks to Ella Brown for handcrafted cards that adorned my office as I worked.

A special thanks to ALL my BPTC law students at City, University of London for the privilege of sharing their many achievements.

Internal formatting and arrangement by Chad Robertson, www.writingnights.org

Book covers designed by Vanessa Mendozzi, Graphic designer www.vanessamendozzidesign.com

Printed in Great Britain
by Amazon

29713821R00084